Old Ranfurly

drew mckenzie

Published by

The Old Course Ranfurly Golf Club Limited
2005

I.S.B.N. No 0-9551634-0-4

978-0-9551634-0-1

Cover: The Original First Green

Contents

Having been a member of the Old Course Ranfurly Golf Club for over thirty years it is indeed a great privilege for me to have served as Club Captain in this our Centenary Year.

We have had a wonderful year of celebration and through this book we pay tribute to those that have contributed so much to the well being of the Club throughout the years and my sincere thanks go to its author Drew McKenzie.

My thanks also extend to my Board of Directors, to the Centenary Committee and to so many individuals for all the fine work that has been done in making this year such a success.

Our Centenary has created a spirit of enthusiasm and pride within the club which I am sure will endure long after the celebrations end.

George L MacDougall

Captain

The Golf Clubs of Bridge of Weir

A brief outline of the development of the game in the village

1889 Ranfurly Castle Golf Club formed and played over nine holes at Brannochlie. This is the area of land now covered by the 'inside eight' at Old Ranfurly.

1894 The course was extended to eighteen holes incorporating the land of Shillingworth and Whinnerstone.

1896 Bridge of Weir Golf Club was formed and played over nine holes at a rough area of ground between Lochend and Barnbeth. The course lasted only a few years.

1896 Bridge of Weir and Ranfurly Ladies Golf Club formed and played over a picturesque nine holes at Horsewood.

1899 The Thistle Golf Club formed and played over nine holes at Clevans.

1904 The Thistle Golf Club move to Auchensale on account of the land at Clevans having been purchased by the Ranfurly Castle Golf Club.

1905 Ranfurly Castle Golf Club move location to Clevans.

1905 The Old Course Ranfurly Golf Club is formed for the continuance of the game over the course previously occupied by Ranfurly Castle Golf Club.

1906 The Bridge of Weir and Ranfurly Ladies Golf Club relocate from Horsewood to nine holes at Clevans on land owned by and adjacent to Ranfurly Castle Golf Club.

1914 The Thistle Golf Club closed with the onset of the Great War.

1915 The Ladies Golf Club closed.

1925 The Thistle Golf Club re-opened.

1939 The Thistle Golf Club closed.

1948 The Thistle Golf Club is re-opened with a new 10 year lease.

1958 The Thistle Golf Club goes out of existence.

1989 The Ranfurly Castle Golf Club celebrated its centenary.

2005 The Old Course Ranfurly Golf Club celebrates its centenary.

Ranfurly

'Than Ranfurly, there is probably no prettier village situated within such easy reach of Glasgow. Situated in Strathgryffe, the valley of the River Gryffe, it nestles on the hillside - a quiet, rural retreat, set amid scenery of the most beautiful description. Its breezy uplands are unsullied by the smoke of any factory chimney, and the air has that peculiarly pure and mountain-like quality which medical men consider to be so much superior to the stronger and more relaxing air that the coast supplies. Yet those who seek ozone find it in Ranfurly, for the winds that flit over the Ayrshire hills, come fresh from the sea, only tempered by the magic influence of the moorland over which they sweep.'

Is it any wonder that when Queen Victoria was considering a Scottish seat, her medical advisors recommended three possible places: Balmoral, Rothesay or Ranfurly?

Ranfurly - the name means 'portion of the farthing rental', coming from the Gaelic rann, meaning part or portion and feorlinn, meaning farthing. The name Ranfurly is older than that of Bridge of Weir, the latter not being mentioned in the poll tax roll of 1695. Later they were often referred to in official documents as being adjoining villages but were actually situated in different Parishes, Bridge of Weir in Houston Parish and Ranfurly falling within Kilbarchan Parish, the divide being the River Gryffe.

James Watt of Ranfurly, who died in 1839, must indeed have been a colourful character. Being the Provost of Greenock between 1834 and 1837, he is often confused with the famous engineer and steam engine developer of the same name who also hailed from that town. His family had originally come from Stranraer and he was a cooper to trade. He had been employed by a company in Paisley by the name of Fairley...who are mentioned now as having been distillers and smugglers. Mr Ramsay, a brewer, afterwards employed him in the same town, and Watt had the very good sense to marry his daughter.

At the beginning of the 1800s he acquired from the widow of Alexander Knox an established brewery in the East End of Greenock at Crawfurdsdyke. This proved to be lucrative. He brewed beer for export to the West Indies, which was sent out in barrels. The barrels, in turn, being replenished with sugar and sent back to the Brewery. A large part of his accumulated fortune was in due course invested in the land and property at Ranfurly. In 1838, Watt's daughter, Isabella, married the Reverend John James Bonar of Greenock. Their three surviving sons: James, John and Horatius went on to become the trustees of the Bonar Estates and it was with them that the early negotiations regarding the setting up of a golf course took place.

By all reports it is quite evident that the Bonars were keen to see a Golf Course development in the village. In 1882, when Bridge of Weir had all the aspirations of any spa town that you could care to mention, they had opened the magnificent Ranfurly Hotel. They marketed the virtues of the area strongly... the walks, the vistas, the accessibility. After all, the express train took only twenty-two minutes from Glasgow's St Enoch's Station to their adjacent Bridge of Weir Station.

The Hotel itself features significantly in the early years of the village's golfing history. It was within its confines on the evening of Saturday, 3rd August 1889 that a General Meeting was held for those interested in the formation of a Golf Club within the Bridge of Weir district. Agreement was made at this opening meeting that the club would be called the Ranfurly Castle Golf Club and that Dr Henry F. Mudie of Kilbarchan be Captain elect. Sir Archibald C Campbell, Bart. of Blythswood was elected Honorary President and Horatius Bonar, Writer to the Signet and part owner of the land with his two brothers, was elected as Vice President. J Porteous was elected as Secretary and would later also assume the joint role as Treasurer. A committee was also formed to approach a Professional with a view to looking over the land. They approached Willie Campbell.

If any man can lay a claim to have been the principal and most influential course designer of Old Ranfurly it is Willie Campbell of Musselburgh. Well he was certainly the initial one. In 1889 he was consulted by the formation committee of Ranfurly Castle Golf Club to look over their available land and submit a suitability report. Unfortunately, on the evening of the report's consideration, Campbell had the need to absent himself due to a family bereavement but as his submitted assessment had been of such a favourable nature he was instructed to proceed and lay out a nine-hole course, 'to the best advantage', over the land which we now refer to as the 'inside eight'. His services to the Club must have provided satisfaction as the club retained him on his application to take charge of the course and act in a 'Professional' capacity.

Willie Campbell's reputation as a professional golfer was already well established prior to coming to Bridge of Weir. A tall, strapping, quick swinging fellow…never regarded as a sensational driver though long and straight, famed for the use of his mashie, sometimes even putting with it. He had previously served with Charlie Hunter at Prestwick, where, in the Open Championship of 1887, with the title almost secure, he heeled his tee shot at the 16th into a bunker and when taking a nine instead of a four released his grasp of the trophy. The bunker is notoriously known to this day as 'Willie Campbell's Grave'.

However, it was in the world of matchplay rather than strokeplay where Willie Campbell would come into his own. A hard match and a large gallery and he'd be in his glory. How he must have loved the occasion of November 2nd 1889, when to mark the official opening of the Ranfurly Castle course he played that well known Troon Professional and former Open Champion, Willie Fernie, in an exhibition match in front of a large and appreciative gallery containing many of the district's elite. Fernie eventually took the spoils 3&1 and received the modest sum of one guinea for his efforts.

It is amazing to consider that this opening ceremony and exhibition match took place less than three months after that initial meeting within the Ranfurly Hotel. The Club's Honorary President, Sir Archibald Campbell, had been given the honour of hitting the first ball, or rather missing it. However, his fresh air swing was swiftly followed by a sympathetically applauded top and the course was declared open. Despite Sir Archibald being a non-golfer, Lady Campbell offered no solace, 'Man, Archie, ye made a damned fool of yourself the day,' she was heard to utter later.

The good man himself would no doubt have put the day's events down to public duty. He was a Member of Parliament…a bonfire on the summit of the Ranfurly Mound had a few years earlier marked his election. He was a noted astronomer and had been President of the International Exhibition at Kelvingrove in 1888 and would, as Lord Blythswood, discharge the same duty at an even larger event at the same venue in 1901. Perhaps though, he might have been even better noted by a number of the Club's members as being the then current Grand Master Mason of Scotland. Who better to lay such a symbolic foundation stone?

Six months after the course was opened the aspiring Committee staged a Professional Tournament to assist in raising the profile of the Club and to allow its members the opportunity to witness the leading exponents of the day in action. Archie Simpson of Carnoustie won the tournament with 151. Willie Campbell finished fourth in the strong field of twenty-three but at the close of play challenged Ben Sayers to a match for £50. Sayers had been victorious 6 and 5 in a similar challenge the previous year over North Berwick and Prestwick. This time, however, Campbell got his revenge over four rounds of Ranfurly shooting 162 against 172 by Sayers, he then got into a bit of a row with the Committee for not actually telling them what was going on. The Committee itself had been on the receiving end of some barbed criticism about the somewhat autocratic and dictatorial manner that it went about its business. One perturbed member, writing directly to the Paisley and Renfrewshire Gazette, stated that, 'it is an open secret that two-thirds of its members, I am assured, know nothing whatever about the game.'

Campbell's original salary was fixed at £1 per week with the club supplying a workshop and occasional help. The headquarters of the golf club at that time was the old farmhouse at Prieston, which was used previously as the private dwelling house of the ploughman from nearby Brannochlie Farm. Private dwelling house might indeed have been too grand a title for what some reports describe as a 'glorified shed' which Mr Craig, the owner, doubted could ever be made windproof or water tight. The 'house' consisted of two large rooms; one for use by the members and the other put at the disposal of Campbell and his assistants of which there were many. They included David Adams, a golfer of some ability, who blessed with an entrepreneurial spirit went on to set up an establishment in Glasgow for the making and retailing of golf clubs; George Cummings, who emigrated to Canada and won the Canadian Open Championship at Toronto in 1905; Christopher Day, who was the first Professional at Kilmacolm; and Ben Campbell, a golfer of occasional brilliance and who was sometimes cited as hailing from Musselburgh. It is easy to understand the need for such a large number of assistants, when you consider that, unlike any Professional of the present day, Willie Campbell was in complete charge of the upkeep of the course. He attended to the cutting of the fairways and gave minute attention to the preparation of the greens. He would also spend much of his time introducing aspiring members to the mysteries of the game and giving lessons to a continually developing and interested membership and even taking the onus of setting down initial handicaps. He was also called upon, on a number of occasions, to design and layout other new courses - Kilmacolm, originally nine holes but soon extended to eighteen; Machrie Hotel GC on Islay; Cowal in Dunoon; and Seascale in Cumbria being examples. One must understand that golf course design was in those days not the science it is today. Surveyor's instrumentation would rarely be used and one can only smile at the consideration of what those early designers would have made of such things as computer generated visualisations. The designer's tools would have been a sturdy pair of boots, a notebook and an ability in the mind to translate the natural contours of a field into the setting for a dramatic approach shot or the situation of a natural hazard. Campbell's course designs were always of a basic nature and would have tended to be done in only a matter of hours.

Shortly after his appointment to the club his duties were extended to that of Clubmaster for which he received an additional 6/6d (32.5p) per week. His daily tasks were now to include taking in and handing out clubs and looking after the property of members. He also offered a boot cleaning service at tuppence a pair. In 1891, the following year, he put in for a wage increase and was granted a further 5/- (25p) per week but not before the Committee took the opportunity to question him about the current condition of the greens and the lack of golf balls available. Nevertheless, the Committee directed a further three guineas in his direction, as a token of goodwill, to offset his expenses while competing for 'the Championship' at St Andrews but intimated that he would be expected to look after the provision of 'refreshments' at two forthcoming inter-club matches. Oh, how the lot of the Professional golfer has changed!

In the summer of 1892 Campbell knocked it round Ranfurly in a creditable 33 to set a new course record. He found himself busy at this time receiving entries and preparing the course for the Autumn Professional Tournament which, with a prize pool of £25, was exactly what was on offer at the Open Championship. The first prize of £8 was won comfortably by Willie Park Jnr whose four round total of 141 included a 34 for the first round and a 33 for the last, beating Sandy Herd into second place by a margin of 12 shots. Unfortunately Willie Campbell finished well down the list on this occasion.

At the end of 1892 a new clubhouse was opened and Campbell was provided with a workshop at the rear of the building. His wages were extended to 25/- (£1.25) per week with a weekly bonus of 5/- (25p) to be paid quarterly. In return he was to attend to the lighting of fires and gas and oil lamps and guarantee the continuing provision of an adequate supply of golf balls. It was around this time alas that Campbell started to fall out of favour with the Club. Some members complained that he was often found seated in the Club Room and was disrespectful and over familiar at times. Reading

BARNGILL BRIDGE OF WEIR

between the lines there were no doubt clashes of personality and with these shortcomings eventually being brought to his attention, Campbell resigned in August of 1893.

In 1894 he emigrated to the United States where he was unfortunate to lose in what has become regarded as the first, albeit unofficial, U.S. Open Championship by two holes to Willie Dunn over the Shinnecock Hills course in New York. He became the Professional to The Country Club, Brookline, Massachusetts where he undertook the extension of their course from six to nine holes incorporating a replica of the 'Redan' hole from the West Links, North Berwick. He went on to plan and layout many other courses in the Northeast of his adopted country but found his health starting to fail. He succumbed to a rheumatic condition in 1900 at the age of thirty-eight. His wife Georgina, who also came from Musselburgh, went on to make her own name in the golfing world and is often regarded as being America's first female Professional.

In March 1890, a lease was drawn up between Alexander McPherson, who was the tenant of the farm of Brannochlie and Prieston, the trustees of the late James Watt of Ranfurly (the Bonars) and the Ranfurly Castle Golf Club. Within the amalgam of legal stipulations and get out clauses, the Bonars agreed to build a wall around the confines of the Castle ruin and to wire fence the boundaries of the course, the cost of which would be borne by the club throughout the tenure of the lease. They also maintained the shooting rights of the land while Farmer McPherson was given the right to graze sheep and up to ten milking cows, as well as being allowed to top dress with lime any portion of the land not being used for golf.

The ruins of Ranfurly Castle before any golf course

The Ranfurly Hotel

The building was designed by Robert Raeburn and James Miller and still stands today as desirable residential flats with shop premises below. It is a fine example of the Scottish Baronial style of architecture but only actually served as a hotel between 1882 and 1914. During the First World War it was used as a hostel for Belgian Nationals who had been forced to flee their homeland. In 1918 it became the Ranfurly Auxiliary Hospital and was a rehabilitation centre for around eighty wounded soldiers returning from the hostilities. In 1920 it became the Ranfurly Castle School, having being acquired by two graduate demobilised army officers, Captains C. K. Cotton and W. L. Dudley. The former was a leading golfer at Ranfurly Castle and was champion there in 1923. The school operated for only five years before being taken over by Mr Barr from Kilmacolm who converted it into the shops and houses as at present.

The Other Clubs and Courses . . .

Bridge of Weir Golf Club was formed in 1896 and played over 9 holes on a rough area of land quite removed from the village between Lochend Farm and Barnbeth, the area to the right of the present fourteenth hole at Ranfurly Castle. The Club had been set up by twelve men of the district who styled themselves as 'Proprietary Members' and who, when setting up the constitution of the Club, ensured that their own personal rights and privileges were just a little superior to that of the Ordinary Member.

Even George Orwell would have struggled to have come up with a better rule than Rule 7. It stated - 'Proprietary Members reserve the right to modify, repeal or add to the foregoing as they think fit', which is perhaps another way of saying that the first six rules were really just for show. It is understandable why the 'Twelve Apostles' came to take some good-natured ribbing around the district.

In what does appear to have been a rather autocratic set up, it is not surprising that there would be eventual rumblings of discontent and within three years a large number of members were leaving to join a new club with a new name playing over the farmland at Clevans. This was to be the Thistle Golf Club. The course at Lochend would fade shortly afterwards into oblivion while the actual Bridge of Weir Golf Club would survive for many years as a 'club within a club' and play regular matches over the various courses in the village.

Early Bridge of Weir

The opening ceremony at the new Bridge of Weir and Ranfurly Ladies Golf Clubhouse by Lady Spiers of Elderslie – 16th October 1897

Bridge of Weir and Ranfurly Ladies Golf Club was formed in 1896. Ranfurly Castle Golf Club had already been in existence for seven years but in that period the members had shown neither the will nor the inclination to admit ladies amongst their numbers.

The ladies of the district, far from being outdone, took matters, as they are always prone to do, into their own hands and entered into a lease on a rather beautifully situated parcel of land at Horsewood which was owned by a Miss Finlay.

In fairness, they were greatly assisted in their endeavours to lay out their new course and put it in order by the gentlemen of Ranfurly Castle and it was that Club's Immediate Past Captain, John Sangster, who formally declared the course open. In his opening remarks he said, 'Two courses already exist for gentlemen (Ranfurly Castle and Lochend) and it is a great pleasure to introduce a third, this time for ladies'. Over one hundred ladies comprised the opening membership and they must have extracted great pleasure when after the opening ceremony, in a lovely piece of gender reversal, Mr Nicholson, husband of the first Captain, drove off the first ball.

The Ladies Club was to remain at this location until 1905 when it became apparent that, due to the boom in house building and the desirability of the land on which their course was situated, their lease was unlikely to be renewed. They decided therefore that it was in their best interest to accept the offer from Ranfurly Castle Golf Club to lease from them a distinct portion of their newly purchased land at Clevans.

They commenced playing over a course situated adjacent to the 'New' Ranfurly course in May 1906. An up to date clubhouse, complete with veranda, was erected for them some sixty yards below Clevans Farm.

William Lyle recorded for us a brief description of the course: -

The length of the nine-hole course was a few yards over a mile, and the first two holes, each two hundred and fifty yards long, ran parallel with the last two of the Ranfurly Club. The third hole was across the Barnbeth Road and the fourth ran down to the valley of the Powburn, near Cauldside, an old farmhouse no longer in existence. Returning uphill the fifth green was on a plateau, which provided a lot of amusement for those who pitched too far or too wide. The sixth hole provided no hazards for the good or moderate players. Re-crossing the road again were the three home holes running alongside Barnbeth Road, one of them seventy-five yards, and the last and longest, three hundred yards downhill.'

Many of the distinguished ladies of the district were active members of the Club: Lady Anne Spiers, Lady Glen-Coats of Paisley, Mrs J.G.Cunninghame of Craigends and Mrs John McNab of Howwood. All of whom were interested and involved in the affairs of the Club rather than, one might suspect, being merely figureheads.

As the years went by, the Ladies Club, probably no doubt due to their situation, became regarded as being connected with Ranfurly Castle Golf Club and in due course was eventually integrated into that body.

The Thistle Golf Club, for the first few years of its existence, played over the land at Clevans. It was officially opened in May 1899 by Mr Charles Bine-Renshaw MP of Barochan who, in his opening remarks, acknowledged that although the club could be regarded as a working man's institution, it indeed boasted two Members of Parliament within its ranks.

In 1901, the President of the club was an Edward McBain but perhaps more interestingly the Captain was James Cuthbertson who was to find himself four years later as Captain of 'New Ranfurly', driving off the first ball.

In 1903 the Thistle club struck a deal with Mr Collins, of printing and publishing fame, where they agreed to accept one hundred of his employees as part-time members who were entitled to play on a Saturday only. The annual fee for these members was set at 10/- for gentlemen and 5/- for ladies. Mr Collins was duly elected Captain, a position he held for two years.

By the end of 1903, the Thistle Club's tenure on the land at Clevans had drawn to a close due to Ranfurly Castle Golf Club having purchased the land. Alternative arrangements were well in hand however, and within a year the Club was well settled at Auchensale, near the Farl o' Breid.

A card from the Thistle Course

A pavilion of reasonable distinction was erected and the Club was to enjoy a settled period despite a short lived attempt of extending to eighteen holes. However, the First World War was to bring closure and the course remained closed until 1925. The re-opening ceremony was conducted with great occasion. Mrs Arthur Muirhead drove off the first ball and was duly presented with a suitably inscribed silver mounted club that had been made by James Andrew, the former Professional at Old Ranfurly. An exhibition match duly followed, featuring Scottish Internationalist John Caven of Cochrane Castle and John Anderson, the Old Ranfurly champion. They were pitted against the renowned Glasgow pairing of John Brodie and William Tulloch, who were to take the eventual spoils. At the close of play, Mr Arthur Muirhead presented each player with a pocket book of Bridge of Weir leather.

Mr Muirhead, himself a Past-Captain at Old Ranfurly, was indeed, personally and through his company, a great and continual benefactor to the Thistle Club in many ways. Many of its members were his employees and he would have had their interests at heart. In 1948, after the club had been closed for the duration of the Second World War it was again the Muirhead family that came to its rescue, acting as sponsors and entering into a ten-year lease with Mr Carruth of Auchensale. At the end of this period, the course was returned to its former agricultural use with the majority of its members continuing their golfing careers at Old Ranfurly.

Caddies

Caddying was big business in Bridge of Weir one hundred years ago. Indeed a thriving industry in the art of bag carrying had developed since the game arrived in the village. Men came from the surrounding villages of Houston and Kilbarchan as well as Bridge of Weir in the hope of securing a bag for the day. It was an assignment perhaps more suited for the ageing youth, those who were between the days of school and apprenticeship, and it was this body that made up the largest number of willing hires, all learning the rudiments and courtesies of the game as they went.

The control and discipline of this mass labour market was in the hands of the Club Professional and it can safely be stated that the human relations and interpersonal skills required in his dealings with those concerned would not constitute the easiest part of his working day. Doing his job properly he would be called upon to use his knowledge of both parties, golfer and caddy, to pair them off appropriately. He would take into account the idiosyncrasies of the individual players; whether they were good payers or tippers; whether they had a temper, were irritable or even downright obnoxious. Conversely the nature of the boy himself would be taken into account to satisfy the Professional that he would be well enough versed in the ways of his temporary employer.

In 1897 a caddy-master was engaged at Ranfurly to keep order. There had been complaints about the caddies playing football and other 'undesirable' games on a portion of the links that had been set aside for their leisure and the Committee advocated the removal from the premises of any unruly individual. There had also been a complaint from the local school board that two boys from Freeland Public School had played truant in order to caddy and it was necessary for the club to give an assurance that there would be no re-occurrence of such shocking behaviour. However, it was the continually re-

A fourball on the first tee. It is interesting to note the diverse nature of the caddies ranging from the young boys to the adolescent to the mature man.

peated melee that took place on the arrival of a train into the station that brought most cause for concern. The boys would gather, loiter even, on a large outcrop of rocks at Gateside, the site where the Clydesdale Bank now stands. There, from the raised vantage point and under the spread branches of a large plane tree that gave shelter from both the sun and the rain accordingly, they engaged in many foolhardy acts of confrontational bravado and goading with innocent passers by.

When the bright summer rays of the summer sun's glory
Caused the loafer and caddy, to seek the cool shade,
And watch with strange feelings, where rich and poor parted,
The rich to the hill, and the poor to the glade.

At the sound of the train, however, the rocks were evacuated in a very hasty manner. This practice of 'rushing' brought with it a number of obvious dangers to all concerned, not least to the golfer himself. When alighting from the carriage, if not knocked down in the stampede he would be immediately put under pressure to make a quick decision, having been met with such a wall of noisy and eager volunteers all offering their services. The eventual handing over of the golfer's equipment was understood by everyone to constitute a contract for the day.

In an attempt to bring the situation under control caddies were classified, licensed and issued with cards with a list of those entitled to carry cards being exhibited in the Clubhouse. They were divided into two classes based on age and experience with the 1st Class being paid a shilling a round while the 2nd Class had to make do with just 9d. Members could recommend a younger boy for promotion to the higher ranks although in practice it does appear that a shilling was the going rate for all those concerned. The potential earnings for an obliging caddie were indeed reasonable when you consider that a golfer from Glasgow was generally good for two rounds on a Saturday. At one shilling per round, a further sixpence each way for the transportation of equipment to and from the station and with the possibility of a tip for the careful cleaning of the iron clubs with emery paper at the end of the day it could soon add up to a profitable day for the young chap concerned. A contribution towards the cost of lunch would also be expected from the golfer and McCombes', the bakers in Ranfurly Terrace, was the source of many such improvised affairs, it being not unknown for a large steak pie to be provided for the hungry warriors. Occasionally a golfer would have his own regular caddie and this was known as a 'set'. In the early evening after the settling of wages, one can only imagine the affluent enthusiasm that would be found in the various tuckshops of the village.

The Castle and the Mound

The ruins of Ranfurly Castle could hardly, by any stretch of the imagination, be considered a tourist attraction, though interestingly enough a search through the internet often leads to reports of visits from the occasional interested party or two, usually having come from some far flung corner of the world.

The ruins are situated on a small circle of land surrounded by the golf course – a parcel of ground that wasn't included in the sale when the course was eventually purchased from the Bonar Estates, and which to this day remains under the ownership of its Trustees.

A fine dry-stone dyke was erected surrounding the enclosure at the opening of the course in 1889 but little remains of that today. Instead, white posts depict out of bounds and a two-stroke penalty for the visiting golfer collecting his ball. Golfers rarely visit for any other reason and any contemplation of ancient architectural design is generally foregone.

The Castle and the Mound, while often referred to and considered at the same time are generally accepted as not being directly historically related. Over the years many opinions have been given and expressed as to both their individual heritages.

The situation and aspect of the Mound is worth a moment's thought. It is not seen from the approach from the Kilmacolm direction. Neither is it seen from the Brookfield approach. From the south it is inconspicuous and a motorist driving in from Houston has difficulty picking it up on the horizon. But stand on top of it and the world opens up…the landscape…the close rolling hills and the distant peaks that form that constant scene…a scene viewed by countless numbers over thousands of years from that self same spot.

Extract from Gazetteer of Scotland 1847

'In the North East of the Parish of Kilbarchan are the ruins of a narrow castle, called Ranfurly or Ramphorlie, anciently the residence of the Knoxes.

About 120 yards South East of this, on an elevated rock, overtopping the castle, is a green mound, all of forced earth, named Castle Hill. It is quadrangular form, the sides facing the four cardinal points.

A trench cut out of the solid rock surrounds its base on the East and part of the North side, & South, the West side rests on the edge of this steep rock.

This mound is 330ft in circumference at its base, 70ft in diameter at the summit, and 20ft high.

The top is hollow. There has been an entrance into it on the Eastern side. This may have been an outpost of the Roman Camp at Paisley, distant 6 miles, of the site of which it commands a full view.'

The notion that the top might be hollow is a lot to take in for anyone who has visited the Mound. No indication of any previous entrance is at all evident nowadays. It would, however, be easy enough to excavate some sort of cave-like shelter within its walls and perhaps that might have been done at some time in the past, although Historic Scotland might have something to say if it was attempted today.

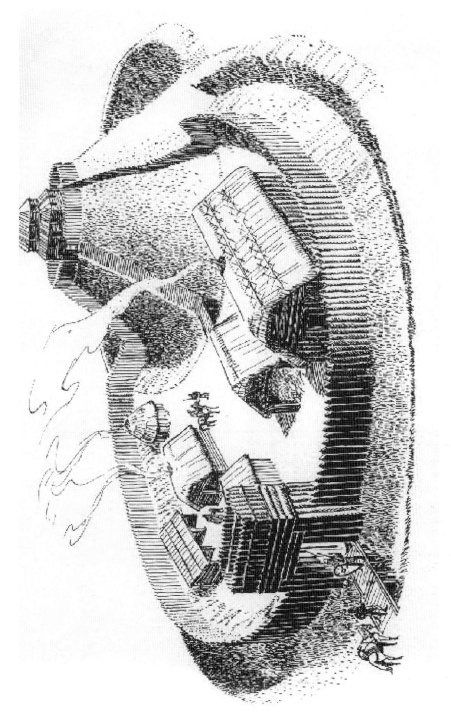

Was a settlement such as this once situated around the Castle Motte on the location of what is now the sixteenth green?

In the late 1980s, the Golf Club's Solicitor, Past Captain Crawford Gilchrist had numerous correspondences with the then Historic Buildings and Monuments Scottish Development Department. This eventually resulted in both the ruins of Ranfurly Castle and the Castle Hill Motte being listed as Scheduled Ancient Monuments. Since that time, the Club have had at least one inspection visit by a government representative, perhaps only to check that the wishes of some members, expressed at more than one A.G.M. and not in any way tongue in cheek, to dynamite the hillside, had not been carried out.

In all seriousness though, the provisions of the scheduling make it an offence to undertake without the Secretary of State's, and one would imagine that it would now be the First Minister's, consent - any demolition, destruction or damage to the structure. Nor are you permitted to repair it (unless immediate health and safety requirements dictate) or add an extension to it. And woe betide anyone who is caught with a metal detector in the vicinity.

While the Gazetteer of Scotland places the Mound in Roman times, Thomas Murdoch in Murdoch's Guide to Ranfurly, issued in 1885, places it much later and he also gives an excellent description of the Castle before the golf course arrived: -

'Ranfurly Castle: - Of the early history of this little fortified house not much is known. Tradition speaks of an earlier castle which the present structure replaced, and in the Tumulus and fosse in the rising ground to the south, we have conclusive evidence of the existence of some fortification.'

Tumulus, according to the Oxford Dictionary means a burial mound while fosse is the name given to a long narrow trench or ditch, especially in a fortification.

'This Tumulus is a very good specimen of an early type family fortalice common in both our own Island and in France, and dating back to the ninth or tenth century. Its construction was primitive but well suited to the requirements of the age, being easily and quickly erected without the aid of skilled labour, and yet sufficiently strong to withstand any engine of warfare which a marauding band of unfriendly neighbours could bring against it.'

This description is historically the most likely and the accompanying drawing depicts how a possible encampment may have looked with the wooden structure on top of the mound towering over the surrounding countryside.

Murdoch goes on to describe the current ruin: -
'All the notes of the district as far back as they are known to exist, speak of it as a ruin, yet its present state of extreme dilapidation is of comparatively recent date, as aged persons now alive can remember the roof being on the south wing. A cursory glance will show that time has been the most gentle of the ravagers who have assailed the walls. Freestone being somewhat scarce in the district, the old castle has formed a convenient quarry for those engaged in building operations, and the jambs of door and windows, the corner stones, and every other portion of freestone that ordinary force could wrench from its place have been removed. Of the date of erection little can be said with any degree of certainty. No written records exist and as has been already said, any stone that might have borne a date, or that from its workmanship may have guided the antiquary, has been removed.'

The writer then goes on to rather contradict himself by saying that it would appear that the Keep was the most ancient part and was probably constructed in the early part of the fifteenth century with the

East wing being added probably a couple of hundred years later. He goes on to give an interesting appraisal of what the various apartments of the castle may have been used for and the conditions which the occupants would have had to endure.

But take a walk through the castle ruins if you have the opportunity. Trace the outlines of the rooms through the overgrown carpet of greenery. Wonder about the screams of childbirth that those walls may have heard or think of those that lay on their deathbed within its cold confines. Imagine the laughter of children at the stream below, the same stream that brought the drinking water and took away the waste. Consider the cultivation of the surrounding land. Think of the people who lived there.

One person, who almost certainly never lived there, contrary to various local legends, was the great Protestant reformer John Knox. His link with the Knox family who purchased the land in 1440 is indeed tenuous. It has been quoted in various sources that he may have had the same grandfather as Andrew Knox who did reside for a time at the Castle but even this has been dismissed as unlikely.

Andrew Knox was indeed another stormy religious figure of the time. He graduated from Glasgow University in 1579 and after receiving his licence to preach took up the post of parish minister at Lochwinnoch. He was translated to Paisley Abbey in 1585. He became Bishop of the Isles in 1605 and was installed as Bishop of Raphoe in Ireland in 1611. It would appear that Andrew Knox was an impulsive and fearless character who dedicated his life to twin purposes, those of the sanctity of the Sabbath and also the continual battle against the forces of Romanism; causes that he seemed to have had no hesitation to defend by the use of physical force.

Just as the link between the Castle and John Knox is extremely difficult to ascertain, so is its link with the Earls of Ranfurly, family name Knox, of New Zealand fame. The main source of a possible link here seems to come from an obscure Irish connection vaguely linking the same Andrew Knox as a possible distant ancestor.

The Golf Course

The Original Layout (1889)

The original nine-hole course occupied the land now recognised as 'the inside eight'. In 1889, that consisted of the best part of the farmlands of Brannochlie. The area formed a rough square with the farmhouse at the North East corner; the crossroads at the West; the Farl o' Breid at the South West and the old Tinker's Wood being within 100 yards of the Southern corner.

The Sport Magazine in 1897 featured the course in one of its editions. We are grateful to the author of the article, who describes in the flowery language of the day what the course was like at that time. From the piece we learn that some things never change: '

The surface naturally presents a contrast to that of the orthodox "links," and grass predominates over sand; in fact, the growth of the former occasionally becomes inconveniently luxuriant, demanding the constant attention of the keeper'.

The tee for the first hole, 'Castle', was originally directly behind 'Woodholm', a house on Prieston Road, now the site of the converted church, opposite the farmhouse which was used temporarily as a Clubhouse. When a proper Clubhouse was erected in 1891 on today's site, the tee was moved directly in front of the new building. The green for the hole was situated in the hollow of the current seven-teenth fairway, in the shadow of the bare ruins of Ranfurly Castle which served as was your line from the tee. In due course, the hole was pushed further back into the clearing that is still in evidence. The rough behind the green must have been heavy as we are told that: *'an excess of zeal may tend to loss of property'*. The green was vacated from the rear and steps climbed to the second tee which was situated on the extreme right hand side of the current first fairway.

The second hole was 'Howe' or 'the Saucer', and the green was situated under the present seventeenth tee, to the left of the now second fairway, before the hill. An inspection of that area still gives an indication as to why the hole would be so named.

The original 7th hole . . . now the 16th

The original 9th/18th hole, now the putting green

The third was 'The Ditch' which was played over undulating countryside to a green situated at the very end and to the extreme right of the current first fairway.

The fourth or 'Farl' is where the excitement really began. The hole ran parallel to the road with the putting surface situated near the present fourteenth tee. The hazards were a low turf dyke and a broad ditch not to mention the out of bounds on the right.

The fifth hole was 'Tinker's Wood' and was almost identical to our present fourteenth. Plans would indicate that the tee was around the situation of the present ladies tee and that the green was slightly more to the right, nearer the road. *'The broken rocky ground on the rise penalising the careless.'*

The sixth is the now fifteenth and at that time was named 'Hades', the underworld, a mythical hell. In reality the most common punishment for the careless sinner was a two-stroke penalty for a visit to the cabbage patch short right of the green, an area which is recorded as having, *'exercised a strong fascination on the gutta'.*

The seventh was the 'Mound' and was the same hole as the now sixteenth but without today's advantage of an elevated tee. It is not recorded if the Club's forefathers regarded it then as their signature hole. One would imagine, as now, it was loved and loathed in equal measure.

The eighth was 'Ravine', the exact same as today's seventeenth. No doubt many of the members of 1889 would share the opinion of many today that it was the best hole on the course.

The tee for the 'Home' hole was situated at the back right of the eighth green and its shape is still very much in evidence today. The flag was to be found on what now serves as the practice putting green. The gardens to the left were always a magnet for wayward tee shots thus being the eventual reason why the hole was duly shortened.

Eighteen Holes (1894)

It was quickly recognised that an extension to eighteen holes would be required sooner rather than later. In 1893 a kind of false start to this advancement was made but, due to an internal dispute within the committee over the unsanctioned development of a curling pond behind the castle ruin and a general insecurity over the initial lease, the planned extension was set aside.

The following year Willie Park Jnr was invited to inspect and report on the lands of Shillingworth, Whinnerstone and Auchensale. He reported in glowing terms but didn't consider Auchensale as worthy as the two former locations, regarding it as too wet with inferior turf. The Ranfurly Castle Club duly entered into lease agreements on the Shillingworth and Whinnerstone sites with annual rents of £30 and £12-10/- respectively. This was formally agreed at the A.G.M. of 1894.

The exact cost of developing the nine new holes was £63 -9-11d plus the wages of the employees. This price included the cost of new gates, bridges, stiles, steps, a new mower and four truckloads of sand.

The Ranfurly Hotel was now able to offer to its guests a golfing haven of considerable appeal:-
'No holiday resort is complete now-a-days without its Golf Course, and Ranfurly is particularly well favoured in this respect. There are three golf courses, the principal of which belongs to Ranfurly Castle Golf Club, which was instituted in 1889, and has a membership of between three and four hundred. It is an eighteen-hole course, the distance between the holes varying in length from 155 to 455 yards, and the course is equal to any inland course in Scotland. Every hole has distinctive features, and with two exceptions the putting greens are undulating. The two longest holes are over 400 yards apart; there is

A party prepare to play the Alps. Driving from the rear of the now 4ᵗʰ green, it is easy to see why you didn't want to leave it short. Note the stairs with the handrail leading to the green

The exhibition match to celebrate the Course being extended to eighteen holes in 1895.
From L to R: - Andrew Kirkaldy, Sandy Herd, Willie Fernie and J.H. Taylor.

one of 350 yards and nine of over 200 yards. The total length of the course is three miles, and the character of the ground is such as to call forth the admiration of all true golfers. The "Alps" and the "Mound" are considered the most sporting holes.

The hazards are rocks, ditches, a quarry, and a deep ravine, which is crossed twice on the round. The course is most picturesquely situated, the ruins of Ranfurly Castle being one of its most striking landmarks.'

Assistance on the tee

Crossing the bridge near the present 5th green

With the opening of eighteen holes the course was played in this manner: -

After the original four opening holes, the road was crossed by means of stiles and the 'Locher' hole awaited. This was basically the same hole as the now fourth, although the dip just before the green seems to have been much steeper in those early days, eventually being graduated in time.

The sixth was the 'Alps'. The tee was twenty or thirty yards from the Locher Burn and the green was situated at the top of the perpendicular bank beyond. Steep steps with a hand-rail led to the putting surface. A topped tee shot, or indeed anything falling short, always found the burn or worse.

The seventh was 'Prospect'. This was a short par 4 along the side of the hill, parallel to the now fifth hole. The hazards were a fir wood to the right, a steep slope to the left and a dry-stone dyke needing to be carried. The name of the hole suggests the view that even today a walk up onto that higher ground provides.

'Prospect'
Putting out on the only hole totally within the Whinnerstone land and the tee shot back down the hill on the original 'Carselaverock' the field of the skylarks.

Sandy Herd watches Willie Fernie address a putt on the 'Home' green. (1895)

The eighth was 'Carselaverock', the field of the skylark, and down from the hill we come. A two hundred and forty yard, bogey 4 hole. The Locher Burn was crossed at half-way and the green was onwards and upwards in line with the situation of the now twelfth tee. An intimidating tee shot indeed with a wooded ravine on the right hand side.

On the Alps...but not quite reaching the summit. Note the bare footed caddy

The ninth was 'Covert' and was almost the same hole as the now sixth. A dry-stone dyke ran across the fairway, *in painfully close proximity to the green*, and the marsh to the right of the fairway did not return the number of balls that the same drained area does today.

The tenth was the 'Dam Hole' and was a short version of today's seventh, the green being situated in the natural hollow. This was the shortest hole on the course and always a possible two.

Teeing off at the 'Dam' hole at a time when it was the ninth

'The Mound' hole looking as problematic as ever.

The eleventh was uphill and played up to a green situated near the rear of the present eleventh championship tee.

The original twelfth tee is still recognisable in the centre of the present tenth fairway near the marker post. This green was where the tenth green is now.

The thirteenth or the 'Road Hole' was one of the trickiest holes on the course. It was played from beside the present tenth green (the tee still being easily identified) across the present eleventh, twelfth and thirteenth fairways to a hog-backed green situated almost at the road. A duck pond had to be avoided as the green was neared. A stile was used for access to the fourteenth and the original five closing holes.

Andrew Kirkaldy watches as reigning Open Champion John H. Taylor putts on Old Ranfurly's last green. (1895)

Putting out on the 'Dam' green.   Down the hill on Carselaverock

Although the plans in this book are presented as the course at a definite date in its history in each case they should be seen as representative of the three eras of Old Ranfurly.

The 1905 plan is as close as current research can come to showing how the course played at the Club's inception and it remained largely unchanged until after the Great War. Photographic and physical evidence indicates that the greens were largely rectangular, the tees likewise, but in most cases we have no idea of their actual dimensions. They are, therefore, mostly conjectural with even the centres of greens unable to be pinned down precisely. This is mainly because, in the case of the 1905 plan, we do not have reliable hole lengths to go on and it is based on a very small contemporary sketch. In the 1920s there was still no, it would appear, codified method of measuring holes. It was still being discussed whether measurements should be from the back of the tee to the middle of the green or from the middle of the tee to the middle of the green. Some "unscrupulous" clubs, in the spirit of misrepresenting their course's length, even measured from the back of the tee to the back of the green! One school of thought was that a hole's length should be measured along the ground until such time as a "severe" undulation was encountered and then "common sense" should prevail. All this, and the fact that if you send two men out separately to measure a hole they will come back with different answers, was not conducive to consistency and is reflected in the fact that every time a new scorecard was produced a few holes at Old Ranfurly altered their length, one way or another, by a few yards.

To establish some consistency all the plans are shown measured from two yards from the back of the tee to the centre of the green.

Fairway widths should be taken with a pinch of salt. We just don't know how they were cut. Since, for much of the early life of the club, they were cut by the local farmer; did he have an idea of how a golf hole should look? Were the holes narrow and framed by thick rough or were large swathes of grass cut and consequently no real definition existed?

How often did golfers enjoy what we would describe as fairways? I suspect we do not appreciate what players of this era had to put up with regarding course conditioning.

The 1930 plan represents the general layout between 1923 and 1934. The areas occupied by the 2nd and

3rd and the 11th and 12th holes had been incorporated with the only changes of note being the lengthening of 11th and 12th from their original teeing grounds, now the ladies' tees, to those illustrated.

In 1935 the course began playing much as it does today. Changes have taken place mainly in the form of tee extensions, bunkering and tree planting. In the interests of clarity, no plantations have been shown.

No attempt has been made to show bunkers in the two older layouts as details of when they were either built or removed is, at best, sketchy. There is no doubt that the course is still a work in progress. In the last 30 years there has been a net loss of six bunkers and much evidence of others still exists, notably on the 4th, 6th, 10th, 11th and 14th holes.

The bogey score of the 1930 course is taken from a contemporary scorecard but the 1905 course was given a total, we know, of 78 and "creative" numbering has had to be employed on the individual holes to match this and cannot, therefore, be regarded as factual.

Several major mysteries remain. On a scorecard used in 1923 the 2nd hole is measured at 265 yards. Even from the old ladies' tee atop the mound there is still a serious shortfall in length. On the same card the 7th hole is presented as 185 yards and the 13th as 145 yards. Was the 7th tee 40 yards back in the ferns or down at the waters edge and was the 13th green where the practice area is today or closer to the 4th ladies' tee? And, if you are very observant, the corner of an old tee can be seen in the middle of the 14th fairway, near the top of the hill, lined up on the area of the 2nd green. No, it's not the old ladies' tee and it doesn't fit any known course.

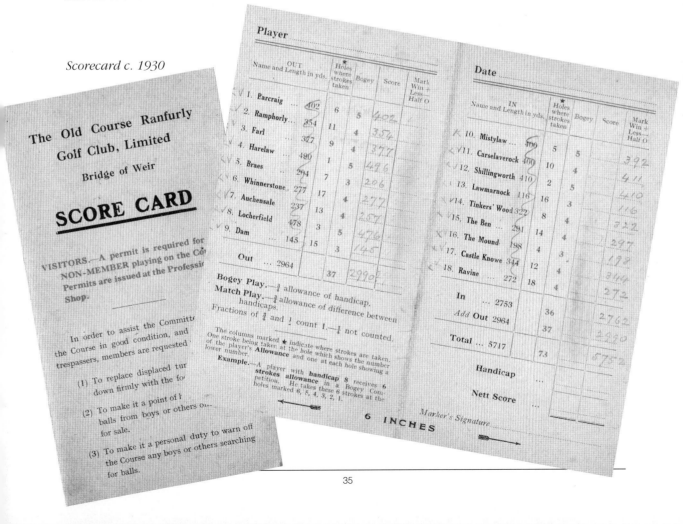

Scorecard c. 1930

Willie Park Jnr

'The laying out of a golf course is by no means a simple task.' So said Willie Park Jnr at the formal presentation of his plans for Sunningdale, an event now acknowledged as representing the beginning of Golf Course architecture being considered a truly recognised profession.

Park designed over 170 courses throughout Europe, America and Canada and was an undoubted pioneer in many modern ideas of Golf Course construction.

He was born in Musselburgh into an already famous golfing family. Willie Park, his father, and Mungo Park, his uncle, had already been Open Champions, his father securing the first ever in 1860, and were known famously for their participation in numerous big money challenge matches.

Willie Jnr, keeping the family tradition alive, secured the Open in 1887 and again in 1889 and took part in probably one of the most famous challenge matches ever when he played Harry Vardon in 1899 over North Berwick and Ganton. Vardon was to prove the stronger over the piece but the first match is remembered more for the fact that it drew a gallery of some 10,000 people to North Berwick, special trains being laid on for the occasion.

Park died in Edinburgh in 1925 at the age of sixty following a severe nervous breakdown incurred through excessive work whilst in America. At Old Ranfurly today, even though only three or four of his original holes still survive (the fourth, the sixth, an extended seventh and towards the green at the tenth), a pride of association still exists between those who now play the course and a man who was one of history's all time golfing giants.

The Split

By the end of 1903, with the name of Ranfurly Castle well established in the golfing world and with the golf course itself reaching a degree of maturation, a decision was made by the Club to up sticks and relocate at Clevans.

To this day, there is still much conjecture as to why this seemingly radical event tran-

Ranfurly Castle Clubhouse 1905

spired and more than a few red herrings have been offered as to the possible reason.

It had nothing to do with Sunday golf as many have suggested. While the Bonars were, of course, sons of the manse and their attitude to this would have been predictable, this particular issue was still really to raise its head and had at the time no prominent lobby within the village.

It had nothing to do with the Curling Club either. A few years earlier, there had been an internal dispute within the Club as to the construction of a curling pond on the west side of the castle ruins. A large number of the members of the Golf Club were also members of the Curling Club and a degree of animosity was felt when numerous fellow members objected to the pond's situation and being. This matter had long since been settled and would have been unlikely to have had any significant influence.

Was it over finance? Well, indirectly yes. There was a great degree of frustration developing in any dealings with the landlords. A new lease was being found impossible to negotiate, despite the Club making what would appear to be a reasonably handsome offer to the Bonar Trust. Yet, when the Superiors came to dealing with the new Club, they were found to be more than accommodating. So money obviously wasn't the simple root of the problem.

Therefore, it is clearly evident that there was a pretty strong clash of personalities somewhere along the line. Though at no time was this ever revealed in a controversial or confrontational way. That could never have been hidden in the village for very long and would have long since been exposed.

The real reason for the split is therefore much simpler and subtler. Is it not quite possible that the leading members of the Club, and remember that we are talking about successful businessmen and wealthy merchants, decided that long term it was in the best interests of their Club if they were masters of their own destiny? There may have been a slight degree of peer resentment as regards the Bonars but that is unlikely. These men had simply the insight and the financial confidence to put their plans into action.

They set about their project with great haste. It required £10,000 to purchase the land and build a clubhouse. The enthusiastic Andrew Kirkaldy was employed together with Willie Auchterlonie to design and lay out the course and in little over a year later the Club Captain, James Cuthbertson, stood on the opening tee and drove off the first ball.

A New Club on an Old Course

On Saturday 21st January 1905 a meeting was held in the Ranfurly Hotel.

It was described in the first official minutes as: - 'A meeting of parties interested in the formation of a golf club for the continuation of the Old Ranfurly Castle Golf Club.'

Sixteen gentlemen were present and Mr John Smith was called to take the chair. A previous informal meeting had already been held where a number of those present were tasked with approaching the powers that be to ascertain on what terms a lease for the golf course might be obtained.

Mr John Macfarlane, a Glasgow solicitor who resided at Kilgraston House and who had assumed the role of clerk for the meeting, was asked to give a report on discussions that had taken place with the landlords Mr Bonar and Mr Craig, and with Mr McPherson, the farmer. As these negotiations had been of a favourable nature, Mr Smith, after much consideration, put forward a motion which was duly seconded and unanimously approved that, 'a club be formed to continue the Old Course'.

The structure of a future committee was discussed and Mr Macfarlane was duly proposed as both Secretary and Treasurer. The matter of admission fees was touched upon and an initial recommendation was put forward that the first two hundred members would pay one guinea each; the next one hundred, two guineas; and the following one hundred, five guineas. The first minute was signed by John Smith.

The Ranfurly Castle (Old Course) Golf Club had now been conceived and an agreement was reached to pay the Ranfurly Castle Golf Club the sum of £300 for the purchase of the clubhouse. A further £50 was paid directly to the proprietors of the land, in order to legally relieve Ranfurly Castle Golf Club of their obligation of restoring the land to its original condition.

Old Ranfurly Castle Golf House, Bridge of Weir

It is interesting to note that the cheque for £300, when presented to the Ranfurly Castle Golf Club, was duly returned not cashed to Mr Macfarlane. The reason being that the Directors of that Club were unhappy at the obvious similarity between the respective titles. The Committee of the new Club then returned briefly to the drawing board and the name, 'The Old Course Ranfurly Golf Club', was duly agreed upon.

A rental agreement was reached with Farmer McPherson who, as existing tenant, was rightfully entitled to sub let the land. The rental was set at £102 per annum plus an additional due payment of two shillings and sixpence (12.5p) per member when the membership exceeded three hundred.

The agreement details that he would also be paid One Pound per year to maintain the boundary fences and he would be entitled to graze sheep and up to twenty milking cows on each part of the land but no horses, bulls or other cattle, young or old. He was to supply a man and a horse as required to cut the grass on the course at the rate of One Shilling an hour.

Mr McPherson demonstrated a kindly benevolence to the infant club in that he offered it the freedom to withhold the rental due to him until it was in a position to pay.

On the 14th June 1905 a letter was sent out to all new listed members that the course was now available for playing over. Twelve days later their new Professional, Ben Sayers Jnr, arrived in the village.

Ben Sayers Jnr

Professional June 1905 - Dec 1905

In June 1905 this advert was placed in 'Golfing', 'The Edinburgh Despatch', The Scotsman' and the 'Glasgow Herald'. An almost immediate response came from twenty-year old Ben Sayers Jnr, of North Berwick, an application that was met with an equally prompt acceptance by the Club.

WANTED
by the Ranfurly Castle (Old Course) Golf Club

Competent Professional
who is a good player, clubmaker and teacher, and can take charge of our eighteen hole course
Apply by letter only, with copies of testimonials
to
John Macfarlane,
98 Bath St, Glasgow,
secretary of the club.

Ben Sayers was already a name well renowned in the world of golf and the newly formed Old Ranfurly Golf Club would bask in a degree of reflected glory. The young man's diminutive father, of the same name, had been for many years a leading protagonist in the world of the big money, challenge match circuit. He was also an ever present participant in the growing number of invitation strokeplay competitions held throughout the country. He sported many International honours but, perhaps a little unfortunately, he was eventually one of the first in the game to be branded with the appendage 'one of the greatest players never to win the Open', playing in every Championship from 1880 to 1923. Not that it is all that likely that he minded too much. He was after all a favourite coach of the gentry and his club and ball manufacturing business had taken off in a big way.

His business was such that by the early 1900s, Ben Sayers and Son were exporting golf clubs to South Africa, Japan, Canada, USA and India and were fast establishing a reputation for innovative club designs. This was now all far removed from the early days when young Ben's mother was the only employee of the company and, while raising a family, she would still manage to manufacture twelve dozen golf balls a day from the kitchen of her house in North Berwick. She would take the round Gutta-percha rods, four feet long and one and a half inches in diameter and mark them with a gauge before cutting them on the guillotine. Each piece was to weigh between twenty-six and a half and twenty-eight penny weights, the heavy ball being used against the wind and the lighter with it.

Arrangements were made by the Committee at Old Ranfurly to have a deputation meet young Sayers from the train and welcome him to the village. An exhibition match was shortly arranged between him and Harry Farr with the new Professional knocking it round in a creditable 72, having taken an eight at the fifth hole (now the fourth).

He was appointed on an initial wage of twenty-five shillings per week. However after only a few weeks in the job he received an approach from the Pittsburg Golf Club in the USA and was offered the position of club-master. It is to his great credit that he declined their offer and perhaps he might have felt a bit peeved that the Committee at Bridge of Weir decided to ignore his suggestion that he might receive an extra five shillings per week until the membership had reached three hundred.

Ben Sayers Jnr remained at Bridge of Weir for only one season, resigning in early December 1905. He went on to serve as Professional at Berlin, Biarritz, Cuckfield and Royal Wimbledon before returning to North Berwick in 1913 to rejoin the family business. He represented Scotland, alongside his father, in the International matches with England between 1906 and 1909. He died in the early 1960s.

When the second Committee Meeting of the Club had been held, Mr John Gray of Airlie was put forward to be Chairman and in turn was duly elected as Captain, a position he held for the first three years of the Club's existence. Was there not something grand and dignified about the way in which in those days men were referred to, in some sort of mild aristocratic manner, by the names of their houses? Airlie is situated near the bottom of Prieston Road. John Gray was highly thought of in the village: he had been a Rice Merchant, with business involvement in Burma and was also at that time the President of Bridge of Weir and Ranfurly Tennis Club. He was a golfer of no mean ability and, through his knowledge of the workings of the game, he was affectionately known to his friends as Mr Golf.

Benefactors to the Club were quick to come forward. Mr McCulloch made a presentation of a Silver Trophy. The Bonar family, the Club's landlords, fittingly donated the Championship Shield while Captain J.R. Ross ensured that his name would continue to be respected at Ranfurly for the next hundred years with the presentation of his trophy. It was also customary at that time for individual members to put up prize money for competitions.

In those first few years of the Club's existence there seemed to be a constant tinkering with all things legal. Mr Macfarlane was despatched to Edinburgh to meet with the landlord's law agents in an attempt to finalise matters smoothly. The Club's Bye-Laws also required early review and some of the changes in them no doubt reflected the wishes of the highly moralistic Superiors: -

> *'On Sundays the game of Golf shall not be played on the Course, and the Club House shall not be opened. Any Member contravening this Rule shall be liable in a penalty of £1 for each contravention.'*
>
> *'Any Ball played off the Course on to any portion of the Lands of Ranfurly not in the Course except the same that are at the time in grass which shall not be held to include hay, or on to any portions of said Lands that have been feud out or into the Castle enclosure, must not be recovered, and is to be treated as a Ball lost off the Course. All persons are prohibited from following such Balls, and from climbing over the walls on or enclosing the Course, steps or openings having been provided for crossing same, under penalty of £1 for each offence. Members are particularly requested to see that this Rule is rigidly enforced.'*

The Club, despite its seemingly rigid penal system, was now being regarded throughout the country as a Golf Course of distinction where a warm welcome would be received and cordial hospitality extended. Visiting parties flocked to Old Ranfurly; railway accessibility was a great thing and a rate of one shilling per visitor ensured popularity.

The Committee tried to ensure that quality on the course was matched by quality in the Clubhouse by personally vetting all suppliers. Schweppes were approved of, as was Perrier. A monthly account was held with Holmes the butcher but it was probably in the choice of whisky provider where the honed taste of the various committee members would be found to be of most value. They requested six different companies to forward a quotation to supply and invited them all to forward samples of their products. The subtle touches of Johnny Walker and Ballantine's were put to the test along with selected others. In the end it was the Mackenzie that prevailed. It was available at 18/- per gallon.

As golf bloomed in Bridge of Weir, an extension to the clubhouse was not only desirous but also rather essential. In order to push in this direction, the Committee decreed that the admission fee would be dropped to only Two Guineas to attract more members, the roll at the time standing at just under three hundred.

Of the membership there was indeed quite a large number of first class golfers with exceptionally low handicaps, some as low as Plus 3. This may have been due to the fact that the Standard Scratch for the course was set at 75, this being the score from which handicaps were set (the bogey or par was 78). Or perhaps it was due to a ruling that had been introduced in order to encourage players to play the last three holes and return medal cards: -

---

NOTICE

Competitors are reminded that failure to return their cards renders them liable to a penalty of one stroke being taken off their handicaps.

Despite the proliferation of low handicaps, there was, as now, the odd bandit in the midst though members were not slow in bringing this to the attention of the Committee:

Mr Robertson was duly cut to 10.

Glasgow 1st Oct 1913

Dear Sir,

I shall be glad if you will bring the matter of Mr C.F.Robertson's handicap before the handicap committee.

When he played with me in the Autumn Meeting his score to the 15th where we stopped was 4 over 4's.

When he played Mr Ferrie on Saturday he finished the last nine holes in 36. He also informed me that he had played our worthy Captain Mr Mingay level and beaten him. A man who is capable of these performances is much too liberally handicapped at 14 and I think he is at least a 4 man.

Yours faithfully,
D.L.MacEwan

Dear Mr Macfarlane,

I am afraid I won't be along in time for the meeting - You might convey my apology - My wife is very ill and the doctor is coming about 8 o' clock. If I can get rid of him in time I will perhaps see you before the meeting is over.

Yours sincerely
H.W.Farr

The dedication of the early committee members however could never be in any doubt as this note duly indicates: -

It was an exciting time at Old Ranfurly. A new clubhouse in the planning not to mention an intended extension of the golf course itself...both visions being kept on hold until a lease extension could be negotiated with the landlords. And then in 1914 just when things were about to happen...other events elsewhere took centre stage.

Cutting the 15th fairway in a most traditionl manner

Tom Watt

(Professional between 1st Jan 1906 - 26th Dec 1907)

Following on from Ben Sayers Jnr was Tom Watt, a native of Bridge of Weir who had been at one time an assistant to Charles McIntosh when the course had been under the auspices of Ranfurly Castle. In 1901 he had left the district to take up the position of assistant at Newcastle Golf Club in Ireland but not before setting a new course record at Ranfurly. He beat the target, which had been set by Sandy Herd in the match that had been played to celebrate the course's extension to eighteen holes in 1895.

'Herd's score has met its fate,
Tom did the round in 68'

He moved eventually from Ireland to Hesketh Golf Club in Southport where he was assistant to the renowned Peter McEwan.

At Ranfurly he was selected from a short list of himself, James Andrew and George P. Elder. The success of his appointment was conveyed to him by a letter, which also outlined clearly the duties of his office.

> Mr Thomas Watt
> Hesketh Golf Course,
> Southport 21st Dec 1905
>
> Dear Sir,
> The Old Course Ranfurly Golf Club
>
> I am instructed to inform you that at a meeting of the committee of this Club held last night you were appointed 'Professional' to the Club on the following terms and conditions:-
> (1)   That the remuneration payable to you by the Club to you shall be 25/- per week.
> (2)   That you will enter on duty not later than 1st January next.
> (3)   That your duties as Professional are those usually performed by Club Professionals in the West of Scotland including these herein mentioned.
> (4)   That without prejudice to what is above stated it will be your duty to see
> (a) that the Putting Greens, Teeing Grounds and whole course generally are kept and maintained in good and satisfactory order and condition
> (b) that all tees are properly set and all holes are properly placed
> (c) that players replace any turf cut out or removed by them in playing and that any player neglecting to do so is reported
> (d) that none but members or properly introduced visitors are allowed to play over the course
> (e) that tickets or vouchers in accordance with the Committee's instructions are issued to daily, weekly and monthly members and their names entered in the books or register of such members before they begin to play and that the sums payable by such members are duly collected for the Club and
> (f) that the telephone call charges for the use of the telephone in the Club House premises are collected and a proper account thereof kept.
> (5)   That you will not absent yourself from duty without the Committee's permission.
> (6)   That you will at all times carry out the instructions of the Committee and make it your business to see that the best interests of the Club are promoted and furthered.
> (7)   That any complaints or reports which you may have to make are to be made to the Captain of the Club or the Convenor or acting Convenor for the time being of the Links Committee.
>
> In order that you have every facility for carrying out the foregoing conditions the Greenkeeper and his assistants or assistant as the case may be will be put under your direction and control and will be required to carry out your instructions in all matters pertaining to the course. I shall be obliged by your letting me hear from you in due course saying that you accept of and concur in the terms of your appointment as above stated and I am
> Yours faithfully,
>
> (sgd) John Macfarlane
> Secy

Watt replied in a brief and humble manner. The letter was dated only one day forward, suggesting that the postal service at that time might just have been a little more efficient than it is now.

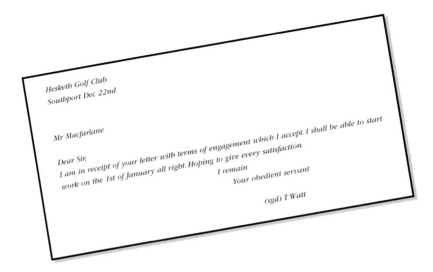

Hesketh Golf Club
Southport Dec 22nd

Mr Macfarlane

Dear Sir,
I am in receipt of your letter with terms of engagement which I accept. I shall be able to start work on the 1st of January all right. Hoping to give every satisfaction.
I remain
Your obedient servant

(sgd) T Watt

To acknowledge Tom Watt's return to Ranfurly a Professional Exhibition Match was arranged almost immediately over the Old Course. Coburn of Erskine shot a winning 83, followed by Watt with an 84. Stewart of Paisley had a 93 with Wright of Ralston taking 94. The scores perhaps indicate that the January weather wasn't at its kindest.

Watt soon established a name for himself as a golfer of some class, challenging all comers to big money, home and home, winner-takes-all matches. In 1906 he won the Glasgow and District Championship at Erskine defeating the home pro George Marling by one stroke. In the same year he caused a minor sensation during the fair holidays when he beat the Old Course record twice in the same day, shooting a 67 in the morning followed by a 66 in the afternoon.

In May 1907 he was selected to play for a Scottish P.G.A. side against Ireland at Portrush. Unusually, selection for the teams was made through the criteria of place of employment rather than place of birth therefore disqualifying the likes of James Braid, Sandy Herd or George Duncan who were all connected to English clubs at the time. Alfred Toogood, on the other hand, was employed at Tranmore and was a regular in the England team. Ireland won by 13 points to 4.

However, Watt must have impressed the selectors with his performance in the Irish match as he was subsequently chosen for the Home International match against England at Hoylake, where he was team mate to his predecessor at Old Ranfurly, Ben Sayers Jnr. This particular match differed somewhat from other Internationals of the time. The usually adopted format was a twelve man team with 18 holes of singles followed by 18 holes of foursomes. In 1907, it was teams of 16 with the match being decided simply by 16 singles matches played over 36 holes. Watt was paired against James G. Sherlock of Oxford, the experienced Englishman, who had two years previously won the opening Professional event held over the new Ranfurly course. Watt found himself one up after a tight first eighteen…it was all square after 27 with Sherlock going one up at the next…the next two holes were halved…then

Watt won three in a row holding on for a famous 3&1 victory. His fine form however did not last until the upcoming Open Championship, unfortunately making an exit in the early rounds.

At the end of 1907 he left to join the Timperley Golf Club in Manchester. He was following in the footsteps of another Scotsman, George Duncan, who was yet to be Open Champion and who was taking up an appointment at Hangar Hill. Watt's friends, through Mr T.S. Brown, presented him with a silver cigarette case and holder and offered him their best wishes as he once again took leave of his home village. He spent seven years at Timperley before being called to service with the Lancashire Fusiliers in 1914.

James Andrew

(Professional from 3rd Feb 1908 - 11th Nov 1911
and from 12th Feb 1920 - 29th April 1922)

When Tom Watt resigned there were twenty-eight applications for the vacant post. After the various references and testimonials had been considered, a short list of three who were considered the most likely to suit the needs of the Club was produced: namely James Andrew, James Thorburn and R Wright from Ralston. The terms and conditions of the position to be the same as Watt had enjoyed.

James Andrew, who was well known to the Committee and had also previously been an assistant to Charles McIntosh at Ranfurly prior to moving to Greenock, was duly appointed. It would appear that the decision was perhaps based more on the decent character of the man and the fact that he was a very fine and respected clubmaker, with a number of examples of his work still surviving today, than on his skill as a golfer. He did manage to achieve third place at the Glasgow and District Championship of 1910 at Douglas Park, Hillfoot where it is interesting to note that fourth place was shared that day by Edward Shedden, a Bridge of Weir lad, who had been assistant at Old Ranfurly to both Ben Sayers Jnr and Tom Watt and whose name can be tragically traced today on the War Memorial at the bottom of Prieston Road.

On leaving Old Ranfurly in 1911, James Andrew was presented with an honorarium of £7-10/- as a goodwill gesture from the Club. During war time service he was severely wounded, but in 1920, with life returning to normal, the Club was of the opinion they could still make good use of his services and re-appointed him as Professional with a role of club and boot cleaning, being in charge of clubs and green fees, acting as starter and other minor duties.

At the start of the 1922 season, however, his second term at the club was brought to an end, possibly through the desire of the club to have a more able bodied golfer in the position. Nonetheless Andrew seems to have had a continued involvement within the golfing community in the village after that time. In 1925 at the re-opening of the Thistle Course, it was a beautiful silver mounted golf club made by him that was presented to Mrs Muirhead to mark the occasion.

John M. Walker

(Professional from 5th Feb 1912 - 15th Nov 1912
and again from 15th May 1919 - 10th Sept 1919)

When James Andrew left in late 1911, forty-eight applicants hoped for the vacant position. A Sub-Committee, formed to see to the appointment, took the slightly unusual step at that time of forwarding to the General Committee a straightforward single recommendation of who should be offered the position as opposed to the usual practice of merely drawing up a short leet for submission. At the subsequent meeting of the General Committee there was a voice of opinion that Mr R Wright of Ralston should in fact be offered the job as opposed to the Sub-Committee recommendation of John M. Walker. On a vote being taken it was Mr Walker who prevailed with Mr Farr and Mr McKillop putting on record that although they hadn't voted for him they would gladly welcome him and support him as if they had. It seems that their objection to him might have been that he was perhaps considered not to be suitably skilled in the art of clubmaking and was certainly less so than his predecessor.

He seemed to bring satisfaction to the members through the way he conducted his duties and a request for an increase in wages not long after his arrival was met with approval. He only remained at Old Ranfurly for the 1912 season before moving to pastures new.

In 1919, as things started to return to normal after the hostilities of the previous years, he re-applied for the newly advertised position and returned from Bathgate where he had been previously employed.

At around this time the General Committee was seriously considering the implications of dividing the job of Professional and Greenkeeper for the first time, the latter always previously having been under the former's control. The job description issued to Walker is quite amusing in the way it was designed to keep him busy. He was to be paid on top of his salary, two and six (12.5p) for each one hour coaching session. He was to be involved in clubmaking and repairing and in the supply of balls. He was to have constant attendance at the clubhouse or on the course. He was to manage all competitions and supervise the caddies. But just to keep him on his toes came the rider - 'in the event of the Professional's time not being fully occupied with the above duties, the Links Committee would consider the question of him working on the course'.

This time his period of employment was even shorter than his first spell, ending in acrimony after a seemingly serious fall out with the Greenkeeper, Mr Carmichael. While the disagreement is formally recorded as a 'misunderstanding', the club did seek legal advice regarding it. Only with Walker paying the club a sum of Three Pounds was the threat of some kind of legal action eventually dropped.

The First World War

During the early months of 1914, few could have envisaged what the next four years were to hold. For some, the peacefulness of Ranfurly would be exchanged for the shellshock of the Somme - the country lanes around Arras would resemble those around Houston, Kilbarchan and Bridge of Weir. Young men of the area who had golfed together were to fight together - and some would die together.

Things were looking good at Old Ranfurly in 1914. Despite long and sometimes tedious negotiations with the Bonar Estates over various adjustments and a possible extension to the current lease, an agreement was eventually reached that seemed to favour all parties concerned. So much so, that at the A.G.M. the Captain moved that the Rev James Bonar, Mr Horatius Bonar, Mr John James Bonar, Mr H. B. Anderson (the factor) and Mr Donald McPherson be all elected as Honorary Members. The erection of a new clubhouse was also very much on the agenda.

Times were changing however. By October, the Club Captain, Mr J. H. McGhee, resigned from office to accept a commission in His Majesty's Forces. The young Club Professional Bert McDougall, his brother George taking over his duties at the Club, closely followed him. The members of Greenock Golf Club were offered the courtesy of Old Ranfurly for the duration of the war as their course was being utilised by the army. Boxes were erected in the clubhouse to give members the opportunity of contributing towards the Prince of Wales Relief Fund or to aid Belgian refugees. All competition entry money was put directly to war related funds without complaint.

By 1915 however, the financial implications of being at war were becoming clear. Any ideas of a new clubhouse would certainly have to wait. There was an obvious cause for concern in the air. In fairness, the Superiors were taking a sympathetic view of the situation but still tended to display an outwardly immovable attitude in their dealings. The members of the Club decided that the best course of action they could follow was to form a Limited Company. Each individual member would have a maximum liability of Three Pounds should everything go pear shaped, but the mood was positive. A new nineteen and a half years lease was finalised and this would include the grazing rights which would mean the removal of fences around the green. The one thing that was needed urgently though was an increase in membership. The entrance fee was dropped and the annual subscription was reduced, perhaps unwisely, to just Thirty Shillings. A letter was sent out to each member forcefully stressing the importance of attracting new blood, putting an emphasis on each individual in the part that he had to play. A further letter was sent out to all individuals who had resigned in the previous two years, some through the uncertainty of the lease, inviting them to return to the fold.

So, at the A.G.M. in 1915, Mr Francis D. Brown became the first Captain of the Club to preside over a Board of Directors rather than a Committee. The meeting also saw the withdrawal of Mr John Macfarlane from his role of Secretary, a position he had held since the Club had been formed. Scenes of emotion were evident as the body of the meeting stood in appreciation of the work of Mr Macfarlane, who was suffering from a terminal illness. His legal knowledge and diligent manner had brought an early stability to Old Ranfurly. He had served the Club for the first four years before they were in a position to reward him for his services - his Bath Street office had often been the setting for many Golf Club meetings, both formal and impromptu. He continued to represent the Club in a legal capacity until his death the following year. His successor was Mr William G. Millar, an ex-champion lightweight boxer.

1916 seemed to start with more confidence, a confidence that would be shattered by the end of the year. Despite the financial problems of the Club, a committee was formed to see in what way they could raise money on behalf of Old Ranfurly for the Red Cross - a fete raised over £120 in one day and was just one highlight of their activities. The Directors, surprisingly perhaps, saw it proper to sanction the playing of the Club Championship. With an entry fee of one shilling, Mathew Barr Jnr was to see off the challenge of only five other rivals.

A burglary at the Clubhouse saw the disappearance of four gallons of whisky, which apparently found a ready market within the village. The perpetrators of the crime were duly brought to justice by the diligence of the local Constable, whose efforts were appreciated by the Club by presenting him with a Sovereign.

To the golfing community of Bridge of Weir, the horrors of war were brought home at the close of the year. News arrived in the village of the deaths of two of its finest young men: the aforementioned Bert McDougall, the Old Ranfurly professional and Robert 'Bobby' Barr, who had been an Assistant Professional at Ranfurly Castle before the war. They had both joined the Highland Light Infantry at the start of the war and both died at the capturing of Beaumont-Hamel, a village in the Department of the Somme, at the Battle of the Ancre. The Paisley and Renfrewshire Gazette paid tribute to both men. It recalls that prior to the war Barr had played six rounds of Ranfurly Castle in one day having an aggregate score of 477. It mentions his pawky good humour.

WELL-KNOWN GOLFER KILLED

PRIVATE ROBERT BARR, H.L.I.

Of Robert McDougall it writes: -

Well known golfer killed

'Amongst the Bridge of Weir men who have given their lives for the Empire is Private Robert McDougall H.L.I.

With a raiding party on Nov 18th he took part in the capture of German Trenches and fell by a sniper's bullet at the close of the action.

As Professional at Old Ranfurly Golf Course, Private McDougall was well known and was very popular. He was always bright and ready to help.

As a player he was very promising; he was deft and was developing a fine power of driving.

In May 1914, he tied for third place in the Paisley and District Professionals Competition in Paisley.

The call of his country appealed to his eager spirit, and in Nov 1914 he joined the H.L.I. and after training at Gailes and Salisbury he proceeded to France in Nov 1915.

He was a good soldier and a staunch friend, and the news of his death was received in his native district with deep sorrow.'

The two men now rest in the Munich Trench British Cemetery at Beaumont-Hamel in France. It took four months, until after a German withdrawal, before their bodies could be buried. They now lie only four graves apart.

WELL-KNOWN GOLFER KILLED

PRIVATE ROBERT B. MACDOUGALL, H.L.I.

The Club granted an application, early in 1917, to the Local Volunteer Force to train over the golf course on Sundays. Besides it being considered a national duty it would have been most surprising if this had been refused at its Captain was no other than W. G. Millar, the Golf Club Secretary.

By 1917, however, financial matters had reached a head. There was an anticipated deficit in the accounts of £481. Membership had fallen to 256, of whom 42 were fighting men and were liable to no fees. The Superiors were not making any signs of being at all flexible and to make matters worse, the Inland Revenue were making an additional, unforeseen claim of £51-10/- against the Club.

An Emergency Meeting was called where it was put that there were four possible solutions to the problem: -

1. A levy of £1-10/- (£1.50) per head be implemented with another possible levy imposed the following year.
2. Money be raised from loans from individual members, to be repaid at an opportune time by ballot. The members to be paid an interest rate of 5%.
3. Money be raised by Voluntary Subscription.
4. Liquidation of the Club.

A Director at the meeting asked the touching, pertinent question: -

'What would the fighting men say when they returned from active service if they found that we had failed to do our bit in keeping the Club in existence?'

After much discussion, it was agreed to invite Voluntary Contributions from the Members and if that failed to raise an appropriate amount then the money would be returned to the donor and the Club put into liquidation.

There was a quiet degree of confidence in the air as a straw poll of those present indicated that about £70 would be pledged from around 20 individuals present. By the next meeting £141 had been received with a further £58 pledged.

The Captain, Mr Brown, the Vice Captain, George Hector, and Mr J. Reid Bennie made the journey to Edinburgh to meet the law agent for the Bonar Estates face to face and to ask for a reduction of £50 in the rent.

The entourage were successful in their appeal, the rent being much reduced for the following three years with a mechanism built in to the agreement that it would increase substantially in the later years of the lease.

The dealings were done with Mrs May Thomson or Bonar, who was the widow of the late Horatius Bonar and was described as proprietrix of the Estate. She reminded the Club that in accordance with the previous agreement, they would have three years from the termination of hostilities to build a new clubhouse.

The Club could now go forward on a level footing and a degree of satisfaction must have been felt when a letter arrived in February 1918 from Mr John Scott, a past director, who was serving with the forces abroad. He congratulated the Directors and Members on their success in keeping the Club going, and hoped that the time would not be far off when he would be able to return to Bridge of Weir and enjoy a game on the links.

Between the Wars

With the 'War to end all Wars' firmly over, the Country looked forward with a new found confidence. The remains of a generation were returning to the fold and plans that had been laid aside were being eagerly taken up again.

At Old Ranfurly, this meant a new Clubhouse. It had already been formally agreed in a previous lease review that the construction of new premises should begin within three years from the end of hostilities. Besides, the old building had seen better days – the roof was in urgent need of repair…not that the rats which were infesting the place minded a bit. A Sub-Committee was formed.

Now, the natural thing for this Sub-Committee to have done would have been to call for the design of the said building to have been offered out to competitive tendering. However, the Club at that time had a member, Mr A. McInnes Gardner, who was an architect of considerable experience and had an excellent reputation and the Committee were of the opinion that the club would be better served by laying the project in his hands. Mr Gardner agreed to submit a plan of a Clubhouse that could, if necessary, be converted into a semi-detached bungalow and which could also be built in sections to suit the relevant financing available.

Plans for new Clubhouse – 1921

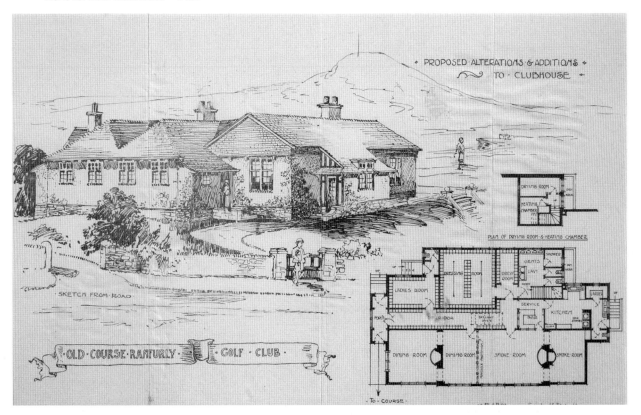

On the question of finance, the estimated cost was between £6,000 and £7,000. The Sub-Committee put forward a host of viable options as to how this could be raised: an increase in annual fees, an increase in joining fees, bazaars and debenture schemes were among their many ideas. The Convenor, George Hector, issued the following two reassuring statements:-

'The committee is of the opinion that new members will be secured and that the increased subscription will not disturb the membership and finally that the necessary effort required to carry out the scheme will be beneficial to the club'

'You will note therefrom that in addition to proper catering facilities, members returning from golf will have the comforts provided by drying-room, hot and cold sprays, suitable dressing rooms, and the conveniences attached to a modern and up-to-date Clubhouse.'

An Extraordinary General Meeting was held towards the end of 1921 in the Religious Institution Rooms, 200 Buchanan St, Glasgow. It is interesting to note just how many of the Club's early meetings were held in Glasgow…in various venues from Masonic Halls to the Ca'dora Building and very often in the private offices of members of Committee. This, on reflection, would not be deemed an unusual state of affairs for of the members at that time…more than half came from the city. A statistical breakdown showed that from a membership of 346, there were 188 regarded as being from Glasgow, 103 from Bridge of Weir and 55 from Paisley.

At the E.G.M., the voice of the Meeting, as it is often wont to do on such occasions, pointed the Club in a slightly different direction and reshaped somewhat the Sub-Committee's ideas. The Members, each of whom had already paid a One Guinea levy, decided thus:-

1. That a further compulsory levy of £5 be payable by each Member.

2. That the required balance be raised by the issuing of Debentures of £5 each with a definite sinking fund being set up for the repayments.

3. To borrow the remaining balance with a loan over the property.

William G. Millar – Secretary 1916 – 1941

The feeling of the meeting was one of unity, so much so that they were even quietly dismissive of a letter from that wisest of counsel, Mr Arthur Muirhead, suggesting that the purchase of the golf course should be considered prior to the funding of a Clubhouse.

So it was full steam ahead. The focus for all the membership was to raise money and the local clergy could not have picked a worse moment to enquire if the Club would see fit to allow them to play at reduced rates. 'Don't think so', or similar words to that effect was the united voice. 'Economy with Efficiency', was the buzzword of the time.

Nine months later John Woodrow, the Builder, had the new structure up. It was opened officially on the 26th August 1922, the occasion being marked by what was billed as an East of Scotland v West of Scotland Challenge Match. The East, represented by G.C. Manford of Luffness New Club and W. J. Guild of the

Murrayfield Club took on the Prestwick duo of Edward Blackwell and John Wilson, the recently crowned Scottish Amateur Champion. With foursomes in the morning and fourball better ball in the afternoon, the East proved decisive winners at both matches despite impressive scoring from all quarters.

With the new Clubhouse now finding great favour with the membership, the suggestion book was full of ideas by which it could be made even better. Some of these proposals were adopted immediately, others died at birth. Others received a quick witted response from the Board. A member requesting the provision of playing cards was informed that these would be dealt with.

With the building project completed and an appraisal being made of the financial situation, it was noted that the take up of the Debenture scheme had been disappointing and the club was burdened with a large bank overdraft. Rumours abounded that the purchase of a Debenture was going to become compulsory. An entirely sensible attitude was then adopted by the Board and at a further Meeting they issued a statement which read:-

'The directors did not want to put undue or compulsive pressure upon anyone – nor to embarrass in the slightest degree any who might find it wholly inconvenient to subscribe.'

When this approach was made clear to the meeting, several members, who had previously formally refrained from a Debenture purchase, spontaneously intimated their willingness to be involved.

To explain the principles of the Debenture issue is quite important. It was, and still is, one of the easiest and straightforward ways for a body, such as a Club, to raise money for capital expenditure. The idea was certainly not new in Bridge of Weir as Ranfurly Castle Golf Club had funded their move to Clevans by the very same method in 1905.

It worked along the lines of Debentures being issued in units of a set amount – in Old Ranfurly's case it was £5. These Debentures, however, were not simply to be regarded as a loan or a gesture of goodwill towards the Club, but rather as a business investment. They paid an annual return of 5% to the bearer but at regular intervals, as funds accumulated, the Club would repay a set number of Certificates and end that particular deal. Who got repaid first was decided by ballot. If a debenture holder had recently died, then it would be arranged for his number to be drawn first and the bargain with his family therefore rendered complete.

In 1924, Mr Arthur Muirhead, the owner of the tannery, became Captain, and with, what was acknowledged as his characteristic modesty and a total absence of fuss, set about applying his business acumen and his beneficent nature to the greater good of the Golf Club. A gift of a flag pole for the Mound was among the first of many worthy gestures. Also his proposal of his son Wilbur for membership was to eventually prove not just a great boon in future years for Old Ranfurly in general but for the golfing world in particular. The young Muirhead would eventually Captain the R&A.

The following year, out of the blue, came the opportunity to purchase the course. An approach had been made by the Bonar Estates and Arthur Muirhead was at the forefront of the discussions. To come so soon after the building of the Clubhouse was not perhaps the ideal timing but with an asking price of £4400 – this didn't include the Whinnerstone land – ways of raising the required money had to be looked at. At an E.G.M. in June 1926 it was decided to levy each member one guinea for each of the next three years, to secure a bond over the land, arrange a further Debenture issue and organise an overdraft facility for the remainder required. It was, however, a magnificent gesture by the Bonar family itself that really swung the decision to proceed when they offered to loan the Club the sum of £2500 at an interest rate of 5½%.

Now suddenly, with ownership of both Clubhouse and Course, the membership felt that they were indeed now masters of their own destiny. The desirability of Sunday golf had been high on the agenda for many years but the religious nature of the previous landlords had always made this an unlikely proposition. In the interests of democracy, a plebiscite of the members was arranged to discover their true feelings on this most controversial of subjects.

The vote went: - For 202, Against 87, Neutral 1.

To placate those who had voted against the decision it was agreed that no bar would be open, with

Bridge of Weir Hockey Club 1927-28
Emphasising the amount of sporting activity within the village at the time – it is interesting to note the prominent golfing connections of many in this picture
A.E. McLeod, W.M. Muirhead, A Mackintosh, I.S. McLeod,
N.L. Scott – J.K. Woodrow (Vice-Captain), J. Alan King (Captain), R.L.H. Frew, G.C.S Hengler
R.R. Elton, I.N. Frew

Four members of Bridge of Weir Curling Club on their victorious return from a tournament in Switzerland in the 1920s. All four members of the rink had very close conections with Old Ranfurly
From left to right: - Adam J. McLeod, Arthur Muirhead, Walter C. S. McGlashan and John Woodrow.

only tea and sandwiches being available. This arrangement was to last almost ten years. Refreshments were then called upon…another vote was taken…it wasn't even close…refreshments were served.

By the end of the twenties there was a definite feeling of professionalism about the running of the Club affairs. Regular stocktaking arrangements were firmly put in place and every avenue where savings could possibly be made was explored. The Links Convenor was asked to look into the argument as to whether it was cheaper to hire a horse and man 'as and when required', or whether it would be better for the Club to have an animal of its own. As it turned out they rented one for six months…but it went and died. The Insurance Company paid out £25 and Forrest, the bone man, chipped in another Pound for the carcase. It was time to consider a tractor. Information had been coming from other Clubs that these mechanical beasts were great labour savers. The figures seemed to show that the upkeep of a vehicle would be no greater than the keep of a horse. The Directors were convinced.

The early Thirties were a boom time at Old Ranfurly; the course had gained markedly in popularity. A course ranger was employed to keep things moving out on the links while at the first tee a 'Pattison's Starting Ball Trough', which was 4ft 6in long and held 30 golf balls was utilised to maintain order. Today, perhaps one of the most surprising things about Old Ranfurly is the distinct lack of a formal starting procedure on non competition days. It is seemingly called the honour system. Two parties arriving at the first tee at the same time should always invite the other to proceed. An obviously slower match should stand aside for a faster one. Consideration should always be given to competitors in recognised club match play competitions and it is always proper that the Club Captain and his playing partners be invited to the head of the queue. The Captain will generally acknowledge the kindness but then politely decline the kind offer. This is the theory anyway.

This golfing boom, however, necessitated the desire for a longer golf course. A minimum of 6000 yards was essential. David Adams was consulted as to where the further 500 yards could be found…and just when every possible option had been considered, the Bonar Estates announced that they would be willing to release a further portion of their land at Shillingworth if the Club were interested. The land, which now hosts the eighth and ninth holes, was available at £250. The Club still owed the Estate £2500 for the initial land purchase and the repayment was duly made in full. The money was borrowed from the Independent Order of Rechabites, an organisation connected with the Temperance Movement, which had great political and social influence at the time.

The purchase of the new land enabled the Club to dispense with the need to continue the lease of the ground at Whinnerstone (on the other side of the burn from the current fifth hole). The work for the two new holes was done 'in house' and it was Mark Seymour, a name that many nowadays might not be familiar with but who was arguably Scotland's leading professional golfer during the thirties, who

The leading lights of the day
(l to r) Mc Auley Stewart (Professional), D Stuart Laughland, J. B. McKinlay, R Niven, John Anderson, J. E. Highton, W. G. Millar (Secy), W. C.S . McGlashan, T. J. Hill (Captain), G .F. Young, J. V. Cunningham, Jas Porteous, A Miller, A M Muirhead, John Pinkerton

advised on the construction of the new greens: - for the ninth he suggested, 'Saucer shaped, longer rather than broad and banked'. The greenkeeper, Dennis Boyle, gave great satisfaction through the quality of his work but was shortly to incur the wrath of the Directors.

Boyle, perhaps unkindly, because by all accounts he was a wonderful greenkeeper, is said to have fitted the bill as an illiterate Irishman. He would walk into the Professional's workshop, put his index finger to the handicap list and enquire what time the next train to Glasgow was. Now, whether someone assisted him in his endeavours is unclear but he sent a letter to a greenkeeping sundries company soliciting a commission for himself on any materials that he might order on behalf of the Club. The company, unfortunately for Boyle, sent the letter straight back to the Board. The Board, in its wisdom, adopted the policy of 'it's better the devil you know' and put it down to naivety more than fraud but warned him that drastic measures would be taken in the event of a repeat.

In June 1935, the golf course, almost as we know it today was ready to be played. The six new holes (5, 6, 7, 8, 9 and 11) had been shaped, accurately measured and were given names to go with their numbers. Major alterations had also taken place in the clubhouse: a new dining room and kitchen, a new Professional's workshop and caddie shelter, increased locker space, a larger smoke room and a new mixed lounge. The formal opening was arranged for Ladies Day. Provost Swan was to be invited to do the honours. A. A. Hagart Speirs of Elderslie was the intended first reserve. Maybe Lord Inverclyde might be free that day or even the Duke of Montrose. The Marquis of Douglas and Clydesdale might have to do at a push. It seemed important to get a big name in for the occasion. As it was, they were all busy and perhaps it was more appropriate that the wife of the Club Captain, Mrs A. G. Brander, should declare, in front of about four hundred people, the new clubhouse open. Her husband, Alastair, who had been at the forefront of the nego-tiations, then drove the first ball on the new course.

After the formalities, an exhibition match was held. J.Morton Dykes Jnr from Helensburgh and Eric McRuvie from Leven, two of the leading amateurs of the day, were the main attractions and were challenged by Old Ranfurly's Walter McLeod and Donald McMaster. Despite excellent play all round it was McRuvie who secured victory for the visitors with a blistering display of golf...he eagled the fourth...drove the new eighth green and despite having three putted from six feet at the fifth still managed the front nine in 35. His individual score of 71 was the new course record target.

A. G. Brander, Captain of Old Ranfurly in 1934. He went on to become Secretary of Royal Troon between 1942 and 1966.

The fine tightrope of economic stability was being constantly walked. With the course now extended more prospective mem-bers were being encouraged to join. Sixty free entry places were put on offer. Ninety-two applied and first come, first served was the rule of thumb but even the slowest thirty-two were offered favourable terms. Another Debenture issue was considered wor-thy and the Club were obviously offering favourable market terms as £3685s worth were immediately taken up.

Although upgrading had taken place in the Clubhouse, it was in its precincts that space was sought. The members needed somewhere to park their new cars. As very often happens in life, an unconnected circumstance led to the answer being found.

The original eighteenth green was what is now the putting green at the side of the Clubhouse. Ramsay Muirhead lived in the first house beneath it. His house was a magnet for golf balls. Long ambitious drives or pulled approach shots often found his home. The erection of tall fenced stanchions did not solve the problem. In May 1936 he arrived at the Clubhouse to pay his fees and in doing so presented the Secretary with a statement, together with a cheque for 19/9d.

The statement showed: - subscription due £4-14-6 less repairs for windows since 1932 £3-14-9. Amount due: - 19/9d. The Secretary was instructed to return the said cheque to Mr Muirhead and to ask for an amended cheque for his full subscription. His point though, had been made. The eighteenth green would be placed just over the ravine and all of a sudden the Club had room for a car park.

The years between the wars were the growth years for Old Ranfurly. In many ways circumstances guided where the Club went, but a lot of consideration must be given to that old saying 'cometh the hour, cometh the man', or in the case of Old Ranfurly, men. The administrative talent and business acumen of the men at the helm can not be underestimated: - Sir James Barr, Arthur Muirhead and A.G. Brander, who went on to be Secretary at Royal Troon from 1942 to 1966, were among those responsible and it would be remiss not to mention John Highton, Captain in 1926, who in 1937 was appointed Under Secretary of State for Scotland, an appointment that Old Ranfurly thought fit to honour with a celebratory function. Only four months later, however, he was dead. Tributes flowed from the great and the good, from all corners of Scotland, but nowhere can it be said that he was in held in more respect than at his golf club.

As the Thirties came to a close, so the shadow of war once again drew a veil over the Country. This would be a different kind of war from the one still fresh in the mind of many members. The lights would go out and for another generation it was time to leave.

George B. Macfarlane

Professional (1922-3)

Both Macfarlane and Ferguson, it would appear, failed to settle in the role of Professional at Old Ranfurly. Macfarlane arrived at a time when golf was starting to boom again after the war and Old Ranfurly was being regarded as a very go ahead and buoyant Club. The Club, it seems, was in desperate need of a starter to bring order at the first tee and this was to be the predominant duty for Mr Macfarlane. Unfortunately the Club had failed to mention this role in their initial contract agreement with him and when he regularly absented himself from the tee to attend to matters in his workshop the Committee objected strongly. It was time for him to move on.

J. D. Ferguson

Professional (1923-5)

J. D. Ferguson lasted a little longer but after a year or so in office he found himself being subject to the concerns of the Board for the manner in which he was carrying out his general duties. He was put on to a two month trial period where he was told an improvement was sought which, as Arthur Muirhead, the Captain informed him, if not forthcoming, 'arrangements would have to be made'. There was, by all accounts, a short term improvement in the situation but the seeds of discontentment had been sown and Ferguson was also soon on his way.

J McAuley Stewart

Professional 1925 – 1930

The tall, angular McAuley Stewart was often referred to by the obviously literary youth of the village as 'Micawber'. As a golfer he was of no particularly outstanding ability and it was, as was so often the case in those days, his skill as a clubmaker that ensured his employment.

He was paid a retainer – a rather poor retainer – of 30/- per week. His workshop trade would supplement that income.

In 1930 the Club decided that due to the amount of expenditure that had been incurred on the development of the golf course savings would have to be made. Stewart was told he could go. Whether the fact that he had just returned from a prolonged period of absence due to illness influenced this decision is difficult to say.

With his ability as a craftsman it would have been most unlikely if he had been out of a job for very long and he was shortly to secure an assistant's place with Tom Fernie at Royal Lytham.

In 1935, a young Walter McLeod left Bridge of Weir to make his International debut. The venue was Royal Lytham. The first person he met was McAuley Stewart.

Leonard Perry

Professional 1930 – 1940

Leonard Perry was a local man. His brother worked in the tannery with Arthur Muirhead. He had been a feature around Old Ranfurly for many years acting as an assistant of sorts to McAuley Stewart and helping Gillen, the Greenkeeper, as the occasion arose.

When McAuley Stewart's tenure came to an end the Club offered Perry his position. He was placed on a rate of only 10/- per week but had the opportunity to increase his income by being responsible for four of the greens on the course. Not having the necessary finance to stock a workshop or maintain a quantity of golf balls the Club helped by financing his enterprise with a monetary loan.

When the war came along and the luxury of employing a Professional was hard to justify, Perry was utilised for a while within the Clubhouse. In early 1940, however, he tendered his resignation. He received the hearty thanks of the Directors of the Club, they purchased his remaining stock and organised a subscription from the Members which raised £10.

The Second World War

Within a few days of Britain declaring war on Germany, Captain Sproul called a Special Meeting to discuss the future policy of the Club.

It is obvious that a good degree of forethought had gone into the decisions taken that evening. The implications of war did not require to be explained to those present. Golf, like football, was once again reduced to being only a game. For the next five or six years both these sports would merely go through the motions, they would tread water and await the time when guiltless passion would be allowed to re-enter.

The Club Championship would be dropped though the other main trophies would be competed for. No prize money or medals would be up for offer, only golf balls. All entry money would go to the Red Cross.

Staff cuts were made immediately, both in the Clubhouse and on the Course. The Professional, Leonard Perry, was offered a retainer with the proviso that he would be also expected to work within the Clubhouse – he decided to move on.

The Course was offered up for sheep grazing…the cattle would soon follow. Parts of the Course would eventually come under the plough.

The membership was soon sorely depleted. Within a year or so around 35 men were on active service, many others were merely displaced by the requirements of war. To counter this, the Club made available Yearly Memberships to encourage anyone who found themselves situated in the area on a temporary basis. Any military personnel based in Bridge of Weir, and there were a number, could play golf for the token rates of one shilling per day and, in a gesture of golfing solidarity, the members of Clydebank Golf Club were offered Associate Membership.

A notice was posted: -

It has been decided to continue without payment of the Annual Subscription for 1940/41 the membership of all members of the Club who are on full time service with His Majesty's Forces and who desire to have this privilege. Members in the Services (or relatives who can furnish the information) should send to me particulars of their unit and rank, by return.

W.G.Millar, Secretary

In 1941, W.G. Miller, the Secretary, died. He had served the Club since 1916. Like his predecessor John Macfarlane he passed away during a time of conflict. One imagines that this break in continuity, at such a crucial time, is perhaps the reason that no memorial to members who were lost in either war now exists within the confines of the Clubhouse. Matthew Barr stood in as Interim Secretary until Harold Walker C.A. took up the role in 1942.

It did not take long before the news of casualties would arrive in the village.

Ian Reyburn was one of over a hundred hands who perished when a German U-boat torpedoed the Escort Destroyer, H.M.S. Exmoor, which was on convoy duty off Lowestoft. He would not be the only Ranfurly man to go down at sea.

The following year, William A. McLachlan, son of Past Captain Dr McLachlan, lost his life while serving as a Lieutenant on the H.M.S. Hermes which was then part of the Eastern Fleet. It was attacked and sunk by Japanese aircraft off the coast of Ceylon. Nine years previously he had reached the final of the British Boys' Championship at Carnoustie where he was defeated 3&2 by the left handed P. B. (Laddie) Lucas. Laddie Lucas, CBE, DSO, DFC would go on to have a life and a half: a Battle of Britain fighter pilot, a Member of Parliament, a Walker Cup Captain, a Fleet Street journalist, a Sports Council administrator and an author. He died in 1998. Consider though the occasion of that 1933 final played out by two young men in the prime of life. Was it not Shakespeare who wrote, 'O God! That one might read the book of fate'?

In 1942, twenty-one men were billeted in the Old Ranfurly Clubhouse. The Club was paid 2/- per night for providing the accommodation. The Ministry of Agriculture supervised the cultivation of the eighth, ninth and part of the eleventh holes. Before the war was over the Club would lose the twelfth fairway as well. They had lost twenty-two acres altogether though had fought hard to keep the fourth hole and therefore, at least, a composite course of sixteen holes could be played. One hole would be played from the eighth tee to the ninth green. Another short hole was from the sixth fairway to the eleventh green and then from the twelfth tee to the thirteenth green.

A tale of both sadness and respect is one pertaining to Dom Coia. He was the owner of two cafés in the village. He was President of the Bowling Club and a member of both the Badminton Club and Old Ranfurly Golf Club. He was as Bridge of Weir as you could make them. When Italy entered the war his café windows were boarded up and the authorities thought fit, despite him having a degree of ill health, to remove him as an enemy alien and he was interned on the Isle of Man. He was welcomed back to the village in 1943, the Board at the Golf Club quickly restoring his rights to membership.

As the start of the war had perhaps been predictable, so the end would be even more so and even by the summer of 1943 post war planning was being confidently discussed. The return to normality was to prove, however, a long drawn out affair. Even by the end of the war those on active service were only returning in their ones and twos. It was 1947 before the Course was returned fully playable for golf and the food rationing would be around for a while yet. But the silverware was once more up for grabs and funnily enough it was the same faces that were grabbing it.

1945 -1960

Normality was returning slowly to the country and to the golf course. Golf balls were becoming more abundant. Meat could be obtained if you knew the butcher and whisky could easily be commandeered if you knew a man who knew a man.

With only 220 Ordinary Members on the books it was imperative that this number should rise. Adverts were placed in the Glasgow Herald and the Paisley Daily Express but to little avail. It would still take a year or two before financial confidence would return for many people.

A serious fire in September 1946 seriously damaged the clubhouse at Ranfurly Castle allowing the members of the Old Course to extend the hand of friendship, opening their doors and making their facilities available to the members of that club.

There were changes in personnel also; Harold Walker resigned as Secretary and was duly thanked for his services at a Presentation Dinner in Glasgow's North British Hotel where he received a grip, made from Bridge of Weir leather, from the Directors and Past Captains. Hugh 'Taffy' McMaster took over his role.

Bobby Graham

Under doctor's orders, one member, R. C. 'Bobby' Graham, was spending a lot more time on the golf course and the practice was certainly paying off. He was winning his fair share of Club trophies off a handicap of 14 and that would soon fall to single figures. The remarkable thing is that Bobby had been a flying instructor in Canada during the war. A plane in which he was flying crash landed and he was buried among the wreckage, his life hung by a thread. Among numerous other injuries he lost an eye and his right arm. The recovery was long and painful, but recover he did and golf was very much part of his rehabilitation. He became Club Captain in 1949 and popular opinion holds that he became a better golfer with one arm than he ever was with two. In 1951, at Prestatyn, he capped it all when he won the British One-Armed Championship, an event much larger and more prestigious than anyone could ever imagine these days, as it was filled predominately with the veterans of two World Wars.

By the time Matt Sim took over as Captain in 1952, the Ministry of Agriculture had at last paid the compensation claim that had been requested for their war time ploughing and the Club was getting well and truly back on its feet. Matt Sim defined the purpose of his time in office as simply, 'to make good, a little better'. Though it was with sadness, on his last night as Captain, when he paid tribute to two stalwarts of Old Ranfurly who had passed away; Sir James Barr, Captain in '21 and '22, and Adam James McLeod, Past Director of the Club, who only six years previously had proudly presented the Club with a silver trophy. The McLeod Cup was to be played for by Category One golfers, in commemoration and celebration of the fact that all his five sons had returned safely from their war time service. The local church received communion chairs from him at the same time.

The 1950s were a time for consolidation despite the various changes of personnel that were taking place. The Club, having had only two Secretaries in its first forty-two years, now had four within a decade. John Hall, who had taken over in 1951 handed over to George Barr a couple of years later, who, in 1960, would pass the baton to the popular banker, if ever such a thing existed, George T. Smith.

In 1953, John Arnott had become Club Champion only a few months before his appointment as Head Greenkeeper, taking over from the retiring Denis Boyle. Arnott had served his time with Boyle and to this day is full of praise for the man, 'he had his methods...he couldnae read nor write and wi'

OLD COURSE RANFURLY GOLF CLUB LIMITED

★

PRICES OF MEALS

Soup	6d.
Meat with Potatoes and Vegetable	1/8
Fish " " "	1/6
Sweet	6d.
Cup of Tea or Coffee	3d.
Cup of Tea with 1 Scone and 1 Pancake or Cake	6d.
Plain Tea with Bread, Butter and Jam, Scones, etc.	1/6

An interesting, if somewhat limited, menu was available within the Clubhouse in 1946. Everything that the hungry golfer could ask for basically, though some did think that the prices were just a bit on the steep side!!!!

measuring things it was always a wee bit of this and a dod o' that and a wee drap o' this…and that's the way we were taught…and that's the way I worked it myself…we're like the cooks wi' their seasoning…ye just get a feel for it…and anyway, that's the Greenkeeper up there', and as he points to the sky he states, in an almost evangelical way, that principal rule of good greenkeeping ; 'just go along wi' him and yer alright'.

John Arnott was to stay at the helm at the Old Course for the next six years before he would be controversially headhunted by Ranfurly Castle. Some members of the Old Course thought the transfer to be unethical, to say the least, perhaps due in some way to the not so subtle approach that had been made by the Castle's Green Convenor at the time. He had driven his car all the way over the course and down to the eighth green where John had been working to see if he wanted the job. The actual reason why the job was available in the first place is also an amusing story: - 'I was reading the trade press', says John, 'and I see this job for a Head Greenkeeper at the Montreal Golf Club in Canada and I think to myself I'm going to find out about this. Now Sam Elliot was the keeper at the Castle…so I go up and ask Sam about it…and he says don't be daft, they awe talk French, ye didnae want to go there…but he wis in for it himself and didnae let on…and he got the job…so when his job came up I took it… basically because there was a house that went with it'. Tommy Fulton, his trusted first assistant at the Old Course, soon joined him at the Castle. Relations between the two Clubs were rather strained for a while.

In 1954, Old Ranfurly had made a bold appointment by naming Hamish Ballingall, one of Scotland's leading tournament players, as its new Club Professional. It also took the time to honour one of its greatest benefactors, Past Captain Arthur Muirhead, who was made Honorary President.

On the course, Leslie McClue and Stewart Murray were winning most of what was domestically on offer. At the same time the likes of Hamilton McInally and Frank Deighton were making the McLeod Cup one of the country's most prestigious to win.

As the Fifties drew to a close, a new generation was coming to the helm; men like Bill Smith and Dan Campbell were in charge. These were guys who could play a bit and knew what was needed out on the course but who also possessed that strength of character and who were able to bond those around them into a team… a team all working for a common aim. Old Ranfurly was booming.

The Swinging Sixties

There was a real 'can do' attitude about Old Ranfurly in the early Sixties…and things were indeed getting done.

Despite a revolving door for Clubmasters…the Banks, the Sharps and the McDougalls all served in quick succession…the Ranfurly Clubhouse was the place to be as regards the local social scene. Who, after all, would want to miss out on the descriptively named 'Monthly Flannel Dance'? The sexually liberated Sixties had definitely arrived in Bridge of Weir.

The qualification for attendance at these wild affairs was, 'Member', 'Member's wife' or 'Member's fiancée'. Member's girlfriends were not seemingly welcome, but that was perhaps a good idea…particularly with his wife going to be there.

Or if it was a boys' night out you fancied there was always the regular 'Smoker'. Could you go to those things and not actually smoke? Was that allowed? Just to go in a sort of passive capacity? All in the days before air conditioning too. Oh dear.

With the burgeoning social life of the village to attend to, this was certainly the correct time to lay down plans for a total revamp and extension to the facilities in the Clubhouse. This had been first mooted by Jack Stevenson in 1958 and future Boards, in typical Golf Club fashion, had progressed the idea thoughtfully…but slowly. It was 1967 before the then Captain, David Gibson, under whose watchful eye the work had been done, was able to declare the extended Clubhouse open. John Woodrow builders were the main contractors and pleasingly delivered well up to time…in the same way as they had done when building the original Clubhouse, seventy-five years earlier.

The cost of the project extended well into five figures and delightfully incorporated many of the modern designs of the age, much being made of the 'ingenious' concealed lighting, the sweeping bar and the various tartan touches.

This was also the era of the 'fruit machine', the 'puggy'. A great deal of discussion took place as to their situation within the Clubhouse, not to mention their moral acceptability. There was a vocal minority against them – one prominent member, John Hall, came out with the immortal quote, 'I don't want my Golf Club to be a chromium plated gin palace bristling with one armed bandits'. Despite all of this, the promise of the undoubted extra revenue easily swayed the decision for their adoption in the end.

And as the Club had fearlessly started to embrace new technology, the next thing was to hire a 'Coloured Television'…the purchase of one would have been a major capital investment with the price being amazingly around double what they cost nearly forty years later.

Out on the Course Archie McAuley, the Head Greenkeeper, was doing a grand job. With regular, paid for advice from the Turf Research Institute at Bingley the course was in terrific condition. More particularly, the greens were in their highest ever order. The Committee, though, were not resting on their laurels. A policy of reducing the rough was introduced. It was to be just the length that a player 'might drop a shot, but not his ball', and of course, this also had the added benefit of speeding up play. Also introduced was a program of tree planting, the purpose of which was eloquently put by Dr Jack

Gibson – 'To better define the limits of the fairways…to beautify the Course…and to highlight the placing of shots'.

And so, just when it seemed everything was going swimmingly, the Club, in September '67, was handed an unsettling double-dunt. Mr Smart, the Clubmaster, and McAuley, the Greenkeeper, out of the blue and quite unconnectedly both handed in their notice in the same week. Mrs Smart was desirous of returning to being a 'normal' housewife while McAuley's reputation was at such a high that £20 per week wasn't going to manage to keep him. Yet another staff recruitment campaign was underway.

As the decade drew to a close John Dunlop, the Club Professional, gave in his notice, and with the best wishes of the Board left to move to pastures new. He was to turn out to be the last regular Professional at Old Ranfurly. He wasn't immediately replaced due to the seemingly high cost of the newly settled regional scale of retainer, being between £600 and £700, coupled with the fact that both shop and workshop required a serious upgrading. It was decided that the investment was beyond the reach of the already financially stretched Club at that moment in time.

In the Clubhouse, however, the membership were beginning to look a much more fashionable and relaxed lot. For the men, 'Ryder Cup' shirts or 'turtle neck' sweaters were now permitted apparel and were for many the order of the day (as long as you had a jacket on as well). While the ladies were no doubt delighted that 'slacks' were now conceded to be acceptable. It might not have been Carnaby St but it was certainly a step in the right direction.

The Newton Shield

Old Ranfurly have been constant participants in the Newton Shield, originally the Paisley and District Golf League, since its inception in 1960. While the wooden spoon has been accommodated on a number of occasions, victory has only been tasted once…on a wet, unpleasant evening in 1967.

Old Ranfurly 16 Ralston 0 was the result that sealed success with one match still remaining. The packed, newly refurbished clubhouse erupted with cheering when the young Stan Briggs gave the thumbs up walking down the hill at the fifteenth having won his match out in the country.

Says Stan, 'The one thing I remember about the evening is that the Captain, Davie Gibson, had brought in a couple of cases of champagne in anticipation of the celebrations. At nineteen, I had yet to develop a taste for the stuff and this didn't go unnoticed by Doc Houston who kept me going on pints as long as he got my champers.'

The scores from that memorable evening were:-

T C Houston beat G G Emerson, 1 up; A Quigg beat J Stothers, 5 and 4;
I Holmes beat B G Stewart, 4 and 3; D Campbell beat J J Aitken, 2 up;
I Hardie beat C Stewart, 5 and 3; J Guy beat D Cross, 1 up;
A Gibson beat G Buchanan, 7 and 6; S Briggs beat D Forsyth, 6 and 5

Post war Pros

John Campbell
Professional 1947 – 1949

John Campbell was a member of a rather unique golfing family. His brother, Colin, was Captain at Ranfurly Castle in 1972. His other brother, Alex, had an artificial leg but would interestingly remove it prior to heading out onto the golf course. He would get around the links with the assistance of a wooden crutch under his arm. When it came to playing his shots, however, he would throw the crutch on the ground and would swing the club while balancing on the one leg. He played off a handicap of eight.

John Campbell, himself, had previously gone to America to seek his fortune in the world of golf. Whilst there, an unfortunate accident was to befall him. He had fallen asleep while smoking a cigarette - alcohol may have been involved here – and he ended up badly burning and seriously damaging both his index finger and the one next to it.

At Old Ranfurly he was extremely popular as a teacher and would seem to have been rather competent in the repairing of golf clubs. He died whilst still appointed by the Club.

Hamish Ballingall
Professional 1955 -1962

John Coia with Hamish Ballingall

James Ewan Graham Ballingall had been prominent on the Scottish Professional circuit for over twenty years before arriving at Old Ranfurly in 1955. He was a Fifer, as an amateur he had won the Fife County Championship as well as securing the championships at the Leven Thistle Club and at Lundin Links.

Indeed it was at Lundin Links, the place of his birth, where he won the Scottish Professional Championship in 1938 while being connected to Balmore. The Second World War, no doubt, deprived him of his peak years but he was still collecting his fair share of prize money well into the 1950s. He took the West of Scotland Professional Championship in 1951 while connected to Buchanan Castle.

He would often be found outside his shop knocking balls onto the fifteenth green and was always happy to participate in a chipping contest for money with anyone prepared to take him on. He was never known to pay out any cash.

On a Wednesday afternoon he could be found taking on the challenge of Dan Campbell and John Houston. Dan explains:-

'He would give us three shots each and we played him for a pound. If he won then we paid out, if we won then no money changed hands. That was the arrangement – we got to play with the Pro and he got the chance to earn some money.'

In fact, Hamish Ballingall's dislike of paying out money is almost legendary. Drew Connell gives an example:-

' My father was caddying for him up at Cowglen in the Coca-Cola, a thirty six hole event, and they're coming off the final green and he shakes hands wi' my faither and says, "thanks a lot Willie, there's the two ba's I played with".

'He also had a machine in his shop – it was like a timer and it was full of red and white balls and you put a tanner in it and it flipped over – and Hamish aye made sure you got a tanner in your change. If you got three white balls in the chute you got three first class balls and if you got three red balls in it you got three second class balls. Most of the time you didnae win anything but I remember one day getting three white balls – and Hamish went pale, I thought he was ill – then he told me that I'd have to pay another 9d because those balls had went up in price that week. It was nae use complaining.'

Hamish Ballingall remained at Old Ranfurly for seven years. He was gruff but he was respected. He once held seventeen Professional Course Records at the same time.

John Dunlop
Professional 1963 – 1969

John Dunlop was the ideal Club Pro: interested, courteous, a patient teacher and a very fine golfer himself, playing regularly on the tournament circuit. He had a reputation for being a very long hitter and he was one of the first golfers of the time to achieve a degree of sponsorship – it was handy having a name like Dunlop.

His father, Dave, was the Professional at Ranfurly Castle and it was with him that he had previously started as an assistant Professional.

In 1969, he moved to take up a position at the new Torrance House Golf Club at East Kilbride. Recently, although retired, he has been involved with the Golf Foundation in that area passing on his skills in teaching children as young as ten the rudiments of the game.

The Seventies

What a mess!!

The Annual General Meeting of 1973 was possibly one of the more interesting in the history of Old Ranfurly though it is certain to say it would not have been the happiest.

Open mouths and looks of amazement. The Membership was bewildered and baffled. It was hard not to have sympathy for the under fire Board.

Basically, the problem was the lack of a proper management system - though one would be promptly introduced. The Secretary/Treasurer at the time, Frank Charteris, a cheery and popular character, was under stress. Business pressures and health problems found him adopting the not unusual, but often unsuccessful, medical technique of burying his head in the sand. Members' subscriptions had not been cashed. Books had not been written up. The financial and membership records were in disarray. Excuses would be made at Board Meeting after Board Meeting for the absence of any up to date report. It was all allowed to go on for far too long. Then that stuff that usually hits the fan, hit it.

Captains all at a Burns' Supper:
L to R – Back, G. T. Smith, W. Wilson, J Stevenson,
Front, J Houston, D Gibson, G MacDonald, J.T. Hodgart (Ranfurly Castle)

It was never a question of fraud, as so often is the case in such situations. It was much more one man's inability to admit it was all far too much for him. The wrath of the members at the meeting was actually aimed much more specifically at the Board for not identifying the situation quicker. The Captain and his fellow Directors eventually pacified the meeting and assured everyone that matters were now fully under control… and just when the body of the hall were starting to come together as one…someone stood up and, in time honoured fashion, mused whether it was right and proper for the Board Members to have preferential tee off times on a Saturday.

Old Ranfurly needed something to get it back on track. Step forward Garnet MacDonald and Drew Connell:-

'We had to do something to get the club back on its feet,' explains Drew.

'Garnet and I were sitting in the clubhouse on a Friday night scratching our heads and we thought of perhaps a Professional Exhibition Match, or more precisely a Challenge Match. David Huish and David Ingram had recently, due to their 1973 records, been selected to represent Scotland in the World Cup. At that time, however, it was widely taken that the best two golfers in Scotland were Brian Barnes and Bernard Gallacher. What if we could get a match between these two pairs?'

'I just went to the call phone in the hallway and got David Huish's phone number and called him up and told him what we were thinking,' says Garnet. 'He was right up for it, especially when we spoke about the appearance money, and he gave me the others' numbers. We ended up having to pay Barnes and Gallacher a bit more but we got the four guys that we were after.'

As it was, it was Huish and Ingram who eventually came out on top. Huish's birdie two at the last winning the match. Bernard Gallacher, personally, shot a 68 which equalled the Professional course record held jointly by Hamish Ballingall, Eric Brown and Bobby Locke. Despite poor weather, more than 2000 spectators had made the day a resounding success. The next year, though, just had to be better.

And it was!

It was billed as a 36 Hole Professional Stroke Play Competition for the Ramphorlie Trophy featuring Ten Top Scottish Professionals. Over 3000 spectators paid to see the action despite the weather, once again, not playing its part.

There was Harry Bannerman, Brian Barnes, Ronnie Shade, Eric Brown, David Huish, David Ingram, David Chillas, G Cunningham, Sam Torrance and Bernard Gallacher.

A Who's Who of Scottish golf indeed.

This line-up was such that if a similar event, with a similar quality field, was to be assembled nowadays it would literally take hundreds of thousands of pounds in appearance money to do so… and that's only in the unlikely event that you could ever find an uncommitted date in the calendar.

Instead, in those innocent days before commercial market values raised their ugly head, the organisers of the event received from each of the participants polite hand written acceptance letters conveying their intention to play.

In a most exciting finish, it was the powerfully-built Barnes who eventually triumphed over the field and collected the £400 first prize with an excellent final back nine of 31, including chipping in at the last, to win by one shot from Sam Torrance.

The next year just had to be better.

But it wasn't!

In 1976 we now had a two day event. We now had an Official P.G.A. Tournament and P.G.A. officials who, while not incompetent, were let's say not as enthusiastic about carrying through with all the organisational detail required. Unfortunately, it was out of the hands of the local organising committee who felt rather powerless. STV were intending to cover the event but this never materialised. Weather wise, it was about the only raw weekend in a glorious summer. The tournament also failed to grab the imagination of the public and the attendance on the course was well down on the previous two years. In fact, how the club failed to lose any money on the whole thing was rather remarkable.

On the playing front it was David Ingram of Dalmahoy who, on his way to victory, set a new Professional course record with a splendid first round 65.

When the dust had settled, the Board at Old Ranfurly came to the conclusion that consideration should be given to returning the event to its original successful one day affair. As it was, the Competition lasted well into the 1980s in the format of a Pro-Am. A glance today over the names taking part in those later events reveal only hints of vague familiarity among the protagonists. It had become an event basically for the journeymen. The Ramphorlie Trophy is currently sleeping in the display cabinet, a font of happy memories.

Charlie Green with the McLeod Cup

More definition was needed on the course. It was decided it needed trees. So trees were got… over one thousand of them. Five hundred Sitka Spruce and five hundred Pine trees went in during the 1970s, under the watchful eye and guidance of Lord Taylor of Gryffe who was well acquainted with the vagaries of their planting.

Lord 'Tom' Taylor was a popular member of Old Ranfurly. His 'Gryffe' trophy is still played for by the under twenty-five year olds. In business he was Chairman of the Cooperative Society, no small under-taking in those days. He lived in the large house behind the seventeenth green, commonly known as "Co' Hall".

A story goes that a golf ball, dreadfully over-hit from the dip in the seventeenth fairway, found its way through his back hall window. It was a 'Spitfire' ball...not the best around at the time. He taped a note around it and posted it to the club. The note said that while he was not too upset about finding the ball resting peacefully on his stairs, he was thoroughly appalled that someone from Old Ranfurly should be actually playing with such a thing!

From l to r starting from the golf bag
Alistair Quigg, Bernard Gallacher, Dan Campbell, George Raeside, David Huish, David Ingram, Garnet MacDonald, Drew Connell, Alan Pratt, Tom Houston and Walter Wilson

One concerned, and particularly scary, comment did come at the 1976 A.G.M. when a member actually stood up and intimated that he was, 'worried about field mice eating trees'. While he might well have been referring to saplings, the words Corporation and Disney do come to mind.

Kenny Bayne became the third Head Greenkeeper of the decade following on the excellent work done by Ken McNiven and then Brian Jones. Kenny Bayne was to shortly oversee the installation of a sprinkler system, or to give it its full title, an Automatically Controlled Irrigation System. This was in and running by 1980 and had cost the Club the sum of £23,622.

An investment of that amount was no small concern for the Club in a decade where inflation was running at hyper levels. This had followed on from the upgrading of the staff accommodation in the Clubhouse at the expense of £28,000. The bulk of this money was raised from a combination of brewery loan, fruit machine income and a debenture scheme that had been well supported by the members.

Brian Barnes

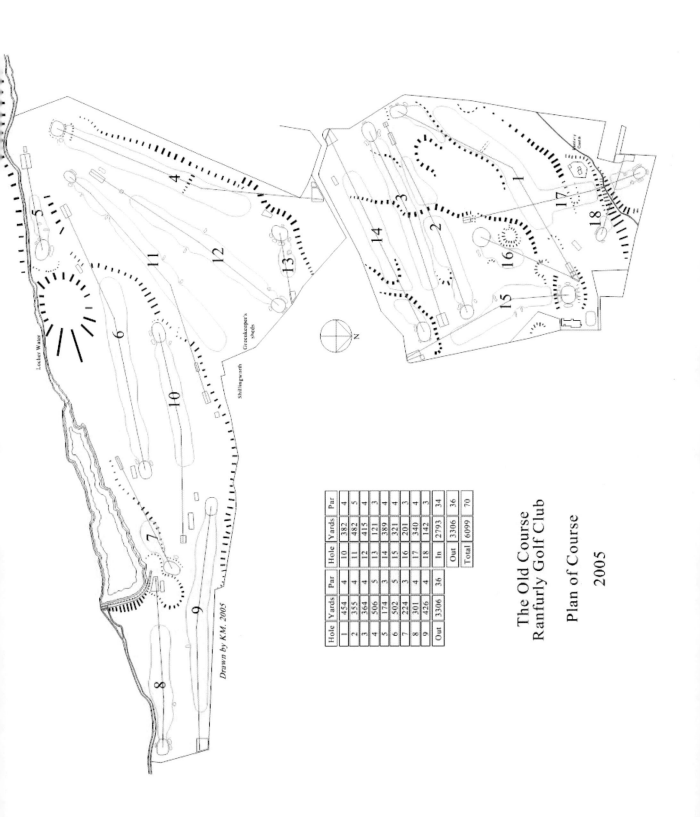

Locher Water

Drawn by K.M. 2005

Shillingworth

Greenkeeper's sheds

Hole	Yards	Par
1	454	4
2	355	4
3	364	4
4	506	5
5	174	3
6	502	5
7	224	3
8	301	4
9	426	4
Out	3306	36

Hole	Yards	Par
10	382	4
11	482	5
12	415	4
13	121	3
14	389	4
15	321	4
16	201	3
17	340	4
18	142	3
In	2793	34
Out	3306	36
Total	6099	70

The Old Course
Ranfurly Golf Club

Plan of Course

2005

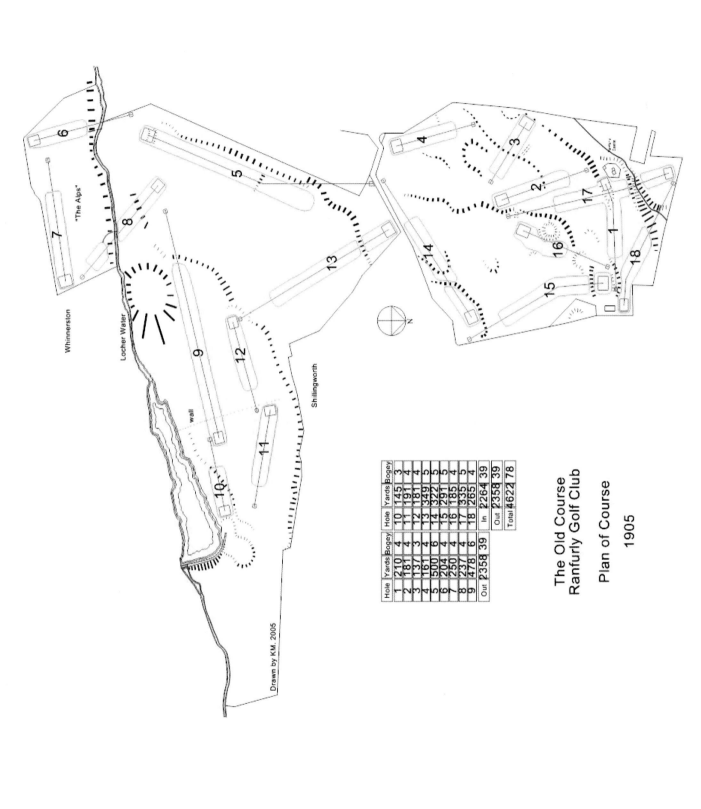

The Old Course
Ranfurly Golf Club

Plan of Course

1905

Drawn by KM. 2005

Whinnerston

"The Alps"

Locher Water

wall

Shillingworth

Hole	Yards	Bogey	Hole	Yards	Bogey
1	210	4	10	145	3
2	181	3	11	91	4
3	137	3	12	181	4
4	161	4	13	349	5
5	500	6	14	322	5
6	204	4	15	291	5
7	250	4	16	185	4
8	237	4	17	335	5
9	478	6	18	265	4
Out	2358	39	In	2264	39
			Out	2358	39
			Total	4622	78

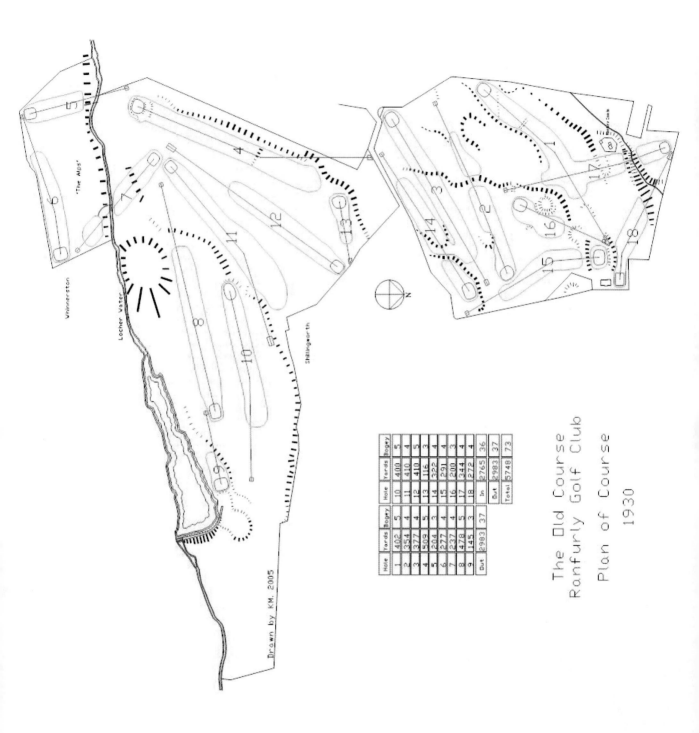

The Old Course
Ranfurly Golf Club
Plan of Course
1930

Drawn by KM. 2005

Hole	Yards	Bogey
1	402	5
2	354	4
3	377	4
4	509	5
5	204	3
6	277	4
7	237	4
8	478	5
9	145	3
Out	2983	37

Hole	Yards	Bogey
10	400	5
11	410	4
12	410	4
13	116	3
14	322	4
15	291	4
16	200	3
17	344	4
18	272	4
In	2765	36
Out	2983	37
Total	5748	73

Past Captains with Captain W.H. O'May 1976

Back (l to r):- John Houston (1966), L.W.T. Martin (1968), Dan Campbell (1960), Walter Wilson (1975), E.G. Cumming (1973), J.C. Osborne (1972), J.C. Smith (1963)

Middle :- G.W. Blyth (1969), J.A. Gibson (1961), J Ross (1970), G.M. Raeside, A.B. Kerr (1964), John Leckie (1971), J Stevenson (1965) W.C. Smith (1959), Sam Millar (1953)

Front :- John S. Judge (1958), A.P. Paton (1955), Wilbur M. Muirhead (1944-5), W. H. O'May (Captain, 1976), J.T. Scott (1946), M.W. Sim (1952), D.M. Gibson (1967)

A Rather Special Past Captain's Dinner

In December 1976, Captain W.H.O'May hosted a dinner for the Past Captains and Directors of Old Ranfurly. He presented each Past Captain with a newly struck badge and thanked each of them for their service to the Club over the years. He then directed a few, good natured, poetic remarks in their direction capturing the characteristics of each for posterity:-

W Wilson (1975)

'When a golfer's wife's a golfer,
What can a golfing
husband do,
But find another golfing husband,
Whose wife's a golfer too.
When a butcher tells you his heart bleeds for his
country
He has in fact no uneasy feeling;
But when a butcher's heart bleeds for his Golf Club,
It bleeds indeed. –
As his vice-captain we laid away problems together –
Which he led to solve –
That other Kojak.'

G.M. Raeside (1974)

'Captain Raeside shed a bitter tear or two,
For awkward things he had to do.
The Greenkeeper chose to take a ride
To a Club way down at West Kilbride.
And problems in the house
That made it clear
The incumbent must quickly disappear.
He got things sorted in the end
And back to normal we did wend.

E.G. Cummings (1973)

'He searched the wine shops up and down
To see what choice there was in town
For Sheriff Irvine Smith you know
Did not drink whisky, but Bordeaux.
A Captain's lot is not an easy one
When Club finances come undone
And Social, House and Greens are chores
I'll wear plus twos and not plus fours.

J.C. Osborne (1972)

The Sec/Treas was missing for most of the term
So Jim put him on the spot at the A.G.M
But it's talk of other things he's done
For instance having holes in one
For he's had to pay the price
Not just the once
But twice.

J.S. Leckie (1971)

John Leckie was the Captain, the year was '71
He planned to plant some trees
Behind green number one.
And as a motion he put forth
The members to agree
He's often won hole number one
But he didn't win one tree.

J Ross (1970)

He's been Captain of the cricket
And he's captained the rugby hurly
And in the army
He became a Captain
Strong and Burly
And damn it, did he not become
Captain of Old Ranfurly
The story doesn't end there
Again he's entered the field
For now he is the Secretary
Of this 'ere Newton Shield

G Blyth (1969)

If you want to insure against a peril
Just contact Gordon Blyth
He'll insure your clubs
He'll insure your life
If you're really keen
He'll insure your wife.
He's served on most committees
He's a versatile chap, ain't 'e?
And on the floor
At the monthly dance
They call him
Billy Daint – ee.

L.W. T. Martin (1968)

I wonder why the audit report
For the year of 69
Was only half its normal length
It's not the usual line
Perhaps it may be partly due
To the Captain in the chair
The accounts of a Chartered Accountant
Must be true and fair
And partly due to another fact
The funds were flowing in spate
The revenue account was showing
A surplus of £7-7-8.

D.M. Gibson (1967)

He annually proclaims a love of thairms
That spew out from a haggis
He loves to garden, an whiles plays golf
And aye recounts the sagas
First Captain in the new extension
And he was clerk of works
They say that there's more Dimple bottles
In the walls that go aroon
Than you could hope tae find
In the loch at Cambeltoon

J Houston (1966)

And here's another drouthy Burns man
John Houston is his name
He's even been club champion
So he's no bad at the game
He also is a medicine man
His patients love his gen
"Take this prescription tae the chemist,
You'll be fine in nae time hen"

J Stevenson (1965)

First of all a master plumber
A master Burns man also
Maybe a master mason too
But that I wouldn't know so
What about the golf club
In this little ditty
And the man who must be master
Convenor of the House Committee

A.B. Kerr (1964)

Ann! Ann! Come quick as you can
There's a fish that talks in the frying pan
"Good God, what a rotten sod
I don't mind being caught
By a chap wi a rod
But what a dirty trick
To be hit on the head
Wi a mashie niblick

J.C. Smith (1963)

And here's another man o' Burns
The first to take the chair
At the supper here in sixty four
You'd hardly think he'd dare
He also is of course
The club's advisor
On matters of the law
What does one do
Bout a lawyer who
Is another Burnsian crone
Perhaps say – but still keep something
To yersel
Ye scarcely tell to any

A Wilson (1962)

It used to be we didn't know
Where water oer the course would flow
Except of course it used to lay
On places where we had to play
A drainage man did come about
And sorted all our problems out
But that was not his only consolation
His was a year of calm consolidation

J.A. Gibson (1961)

Two extroverts are bad enough
But must they be related
Which is David and which Goliath
It's much too complicated
But Jack's a lad you can't ignore
The rules he did expound
The R&A may have writ them
But Jack did them confound

D Campbell (1960)

Dan, Dan, he's our man
He's very keen
To play in the team
He wanted to see
Yet another tee
After four
Where penalties soar
But that's not all
We can recall
He's a great golfer
You all know that
But why does he wear
Such a silly wee hat

W.C. Smith (1959)

I've supervised the juniors
And played the Newton Shield
Been on the County Committee
Represented the club in the field
I've broken par
In my year of office
Seen the departure
Of a secretary
I really cannot understand why
I'm now a plain W.C

J.S. Judge (1958)

Partnerships are commonplace
They're really quite a farce
You find them playing bridge together
You find them on the course
Hall and Miller we understand
Borland / Holmes we don't begrudge
But how the hell do you reconcile
A doctor and a judge

A.P. Paton

They changed the rules some years ago
To make the par more tight
Let's call on Alex Paton then
To put the matter right
They've cut us down to 69
And 70 should stand
I measure with a tape said Alex
Not a rubber band

S Miller (1953)

He's been a member man and boy
Some fifty years can pass
He's seen the day
When real horsepower
Was used to cut the grass
Like all of you
He's served his Club
And worked his fingers bare
He played off scratch
For 20 years
The itch must still be there

M.U. Sim (1952)

Matt Sim has captained other sports
Rugby yes and cricket too
He even tried his hand at tennis
But the game of golf won through
His handicap's been down to four
And that's not just a joke
But his greatest moment came the day
He gave Sam Miller a stroke

R.C. Graham (1947)

He lives among the hills these days
The Cairngorms as his neighbours
He golfs at Boat of Garten now
When resting from his labours
He's picked up cups and medals galore
And he's dissolved a myth
He doesn't theorise about
Which hand to hit the ball with

J.T. Scott (1946)

It's difficult knowing what to say
To a man of 95
It's trite to say when I'm your age
I hope I'm still alive
Your playing days
Must stretch beyond
A time most here remember
The day the present Club was born
You could have been a member

We're proud and pleased
You've come tonight
It's something
We'll remember

W.M. Muirhead (1944/5)

Wilbur Muirhead's done so much
I'm left at the starting post
Captain in 44 and 5
Would be enough for most
British Amateur contender
The Royal and Ancient too
Chairman of their championship committee
That's just one of a few
He even goes to Georgia
That's in the USA
For he's a member of Augusta
Now that's a thing to say
There's not much left
That he can do
Perhaps he doesn't wish
But just to add a little more
He joined
Mach ri han ish

Wilma Aitken arrives at Glasgow Central Station with the British Girls title

Wilma Aitken

Her photograph hangs on the wall of the clubhouse at Old Ranfurly. Some perhaps think that the winning of the British Girls Championship in 1977 is the sole reason that it is there. Some may consider that it was her selection into the 1982 Curtis Cup team, that pinnacle of ladies amateur golf, which warrants the photo's position. Others, especially the young, look at it and see their P.E. teacher at Gryffe High and appreciate that she must have been a decent golfer at one time. Few realise, that for a decade between '75 and '85, how she dominated girls, then ladies, amateur golf not only in the West of Scotland, but beyond.

At fourteen years of age, despite focussing on hockey where she would also gain International honours, her natural golfing ability was quite recognisable to her father's two friends, Andy Gibson and Jim McNeill.

'My father always guided rather than pushed me', says Wilma, 'and that is probably the right way for a parent…it was Andy and Jim that did the pushing. At Ranfurly I took on the boys: Allan Hunter, David and Graeme Conn amongst others - they didn't want to be beaten by a girl. I learned to hit the ball hard. The Ladies Section were tremendous and encouraged me to play in their competitions'.

Though Gibson and McNeill gave that early direction to Wilma's career it was John Semple, the Professional at Erskine, who took on its development. Eventually, when International representation came along, David Huish, the L.G.A. Official Coach took over the reins and when her game was at its peak it was that giant of a golfing mentor, Bob Torrance, who did the tweaking.

A listing of Wilma's more prominent achievements in the game starts with the entry - 1975 Scottish Girls Champion, which she won quite unexpectedly at Leven. Unexpectedly, from the fact that she had only just taken up the game two years previously. This victory established her in the Scottish Girls International Team and brought with it the chance to gain experience and develop her game at a consistently higher level. It was no surprise when she took the Scottish Girls title once again at West Kilbride two years later.

It was, therefore, as Scottish Champion that she went to Formby, Lancashire, in 1977 to compete in the British Girls Championship. There she worked her way through to the final where she met, as though pre-determined, the English Champion, Susan Bamford.

In a match, played in high wind and the occasional heavy shower, Wilma found herself two down after only five holes but by the turn she had it back to square. Her use of the three-wood from the tee, for greater accuracy, was now starting to pay off…she went two up after twelve. Back came Bamford and it was square again by fifteen. The par three sixteenth was crucial. Bamford missed the green. Wilma hit a superb six iron downwind; the ball ended four feet from the pin. She got her two. At the seventeenth she kept her calm and hit the green in regulation. She had two putts to win the match from eighteen feet. The first putt was a nervous six feet short. The second went in the hole.

As the Liverpool train drew into Glasgow Central Station later that evening the eighteen year old stepped from the carriage to a hero's welcome on a full platform. The clubhouse at Old Ranfurly awaited.

Wilma Aitken with the British Girls Trophy accompanied by I to r, Joan Conn, Mary Borland and Grace Campbell

By 1978 she had graduated to the full Scottish International Team. British Team selection would soon follow. She won the Helen Holm, the Scottish Stroke Play Championship, for the first of three occasions and she was runner up in the British Stroke Play Championship. Locally, she won the first of five consecutive Renfrewshire Championships. The West of Scotland Championship was collected for the first time of three. She also made the space each year to collect the Championship at Old Ranfurly. However, it was her success as lowest amateur in the Colgate European L.P.G.A. Championship at Sunningdale that brought her name very much to the fore. On a course playing its full distance and with many of the Professionals struggling Wilma got things off to a bang.

'I remember in my first round I started birdie, birdie, birdie, birdie and was immediately up there on the leaderboard', says Wilma

'I stayed on the leaderboard for the first two days, I was level par, and by the time I was teeing off in the third round Grandstand was just starting its coverage of the event, which was quite a thought.'

Playing at the highest level, against the Professional ranks, seemed to hold no fear for the Kilbarchan girl and it must have given her no end of satisfaction when she participated in the Carlsberg European Professional Championship at Gleddoch House in 1980…and won it.

'I remember the tournament organisers waiting for me at the last green with papers for me to sign professional. I think they were actually embarrassed that an amateur had won it but I just said no, I wasn't ready for it'.

If four birdies in a row at the Colgate were quite an achievement, then the nine in a row at Hamilton to win the Riccarton Rosebowl were truly astonishing. In a round with eleven birdies altogether, the run from the third to the eleventh were enough to merit her a place in the Guinness Book of Records to this day.

'It was all a bit surreal', recollects Wilma

'There were only a couple of long putts involved, everything else was within about six feet or so'.

The resultant 64, ten under par, ensured victory over the two rounds…by only one stroke …from adversary and friend, Belle Robertson.

This unique sub-par achievement is now celebrated annually at Old Ranfurly with the Wilma Aitken Birdie Competition where the prize goes to the person, male or female, who happens to have the most gross birdies on a particular Saturday.

And what does she class as her greatest golfing moment?

'Easy one, being part of the Curtis Cup Team in Denver, Colorado in 1982', replies Wilma immediately.

How often do we find that in the very individually focussed game of golf, that when a top player is asked that question he or she will invariably plump for a team event before any personal triumph? The camaraderie, the additional joint responsibility, the relief and joy of victory, the sharing of despair, the bonding of youth and experience all bring dimensions contrary to the usual solitary purpose of an individual on a golf course.

Wilma's inclusion in the 1982 Curtis Cup Team, after being overlooked two years previously, was well and truly justified when she won the Wentworth Trophy by a clear five shots from a top class international field with a course record score of 66. She also won the Avia Watches Foursomes Tournament at the Berkshire Club of Ascot with partner Angela Uzielli.

As a build up for the Curtis Cup the squad played in the American Amateur Championship at Colorado Springs. The Curtis Cup itself, far from being the one sided anti-climax the score would suggest – it was $14\frac{1}{2}$ to $3\frac{1}{2}$ in favour of the Americans – was for all those who were there, including Wilma's parents Bert and Jean, the experience of a lifetime.

So the big question really in a golfing career filled with so much triumph and perhaps unfulfilled potential is why did she not turn professional? She had, after all, the requisite papers in her hands more than once.

'I had met my husband… I had graduated with my teaching qualifications…I had been playing serious amateur golf for seven years doing lots of travelling, playing in lots of International events…I would wake up every morning and think, "Where am I today?"…Did I really want to do that full time? The answer was always no…and I don't ever regret the decision that I made.'

Now, as Mrs Leburn, Wilma no longer plays competitively. Family life leaves no time for the necessary practice. She quietly gives back to the game from which she derived so much pleasure. She can often be found on practice grounds imparting her knowledge to the young. The Old Ranfurly Ladies occasionally benefit from her advice. She is also about to come to the end of her chairmanship of the West of Scotland Girls Golf Association. Her demeanour in one of calm contentment, she gives the impression of being where she wants to be. No one is more deserving of their photograph on a Golf Club wall.

Habbies in Old Ranfurly

With thanks to Johnny Borland

In 2004, the Habbie Simpson Gowfin' Society held their Silver Jubilee Dinner within the Bowling Club in Kilbarchan. The principal speaker for the evening was the Rev Ian Miller, no stranger to the Parish. The Captain of Old Ranfurly, Andrew Gardner, proposed the toast to the 'Habbies and the Old Course Ranfurly Golf Club'.

Just how far the Kilbarchan connection with Old Ranfurly goes is lost in the mist of antiquity. In the early days, of course, travel between 'Habbieland' and the 'Brig' would be by foot or bike as in 1905. Horse and trap would be an alternative. Trains did not connect the two villages.

Later however, it would be this particular Course that would be the principal choice of the Habbies to indulge their sporting prowess over 18 holes (and the 19th). It fell to Drew Connell to inaugurate a special competition to give the Habbies an opportunity to go out and do battle amongst themselves. For this purpose he purchased a pewter tankard in 1967. The first name to appear on it was Bobby Murdock (the engraver must have been English).

Some place along the line the mantle of organiser fell upon Johnny Borland…being teetotal he was better equipped to 'coont' up the scores at the end of the day. Johnny somewhat expanded the tournament from around 20 players to about 40 and at the same time introduced a prize draw for charity. To date over £6000 has been donated to Erskine Hospital.

As Kilbarchan does not have a Golf Course, Drew and Johnny put their heads together and in an attempt to formalise proceedings came up with the idea for a Golfing Society. All Habbie golfers were sounded out and, as a result, a meeting was convened. It was John Gardner that came up with the name…it had a good old fashioned ring about it, thus befitting the antiquity of the village. Two outings a year were agreed.

It was mooted that the Society should register with the R&A. An approach to that august body pointed them in the direction of the Scottish Golf Union. Information from the S.G.U. did however reveal that too much 'lolly' was going to be involved. The matter was quietly dropped.

In 1983 a Habbie Cup for Junior Members was inaugurated. The following year saw the start of the Borland Trophy (presented by John Borland and his nephew George) which is an annual challenge between the Habbies and Old Ranfurly. In what is an evening of great social conviviality it is not unusual to find the respective team captains doing prior lobbying as to possible team members…many individuals being qualified to play for either side.

One of the highlights of the year is without doubt the Habbie Cup. It is not unknown for the winner of this particular competition to be decided over a sudden death shoot out around the putting green. In the early years of its existence it was the custom to invite John Masson in the guise of Lilias' Day Habbie Simpson to present the prizes. As Habbie did in days of old he entertained the assembly with a selection of wonderful tunes on his bagpipes. On one notable occasion he appeared on his usual route to the Clubhouse, piping over the 15th green…when the sprinklers went off. Alas, there was no camera to record the spectacle. Conspiracy theories are still being discussed.

The Course Today

Former Champion Kenny Morrison reveals the best way to play old Ranfurly.
He also offers his strong personal views about how the course could be improved.

Hole 1   Barcraig   454 yards   Par 4   S. I. 3

It's unlikely, but just possible, that Barcraig is the original hole to be described as requiring "three good shots to get home in two". The playing strategy of no other hole on the course is as influenced by its physical contours and wind direction.   Although the tees are all raised above fairway level the drive will land on a slight upslope limiting the available run. Longer hitters should favour the left half of the fairway, secure in the knowledge that an over tight line will tend to kick to safety. This area also provides the flatter lies and the best direction from which to approach the gently sloping green. Shorter hitters with little or no expectation of getting home in two should favour the middle, or even the right side, of the fairway to avoid any possibility of being blocked by the plantation on the left side of the hole. The decision then has to be made as to whether the diagonal ridge can be carried, to either reach the green or at least afford a sight of it for the next shot, or to lay up leaving a blind approach.

Although little evidence remains the original green site of this hole was in this 'lay up' area just short of the out-of-bounds.

Due to the length of most approach shots the greenside bunkers are not frequently visited and the main function of the two shallow bunkers, that of preventing balls scuttling under George Ford's rose hedge, could be equally performed by semi-rough covered mounds.

Although a difficult par 4 this is a good 'getaway' hole in that it allows players to start on time, due to most not having to wait for the green to clear before playing their second shot, and plays its part as a good 19th hole in matchplay. That is unless you're giving you're opponent a stroke!

Hole 2   Ramphorlie   355 yards   Par 4   S. I. 11

Often played with a helping wind, longer hitters should play for the marker post to leave all areas of the green accessible to a short approach. Any further left than this will probably result in the drive finishing in lush semi-rough with its attendant problems of controlling spin.

The shortest carry from the tee is to the right side of the hole but this line can result in a blind second shot and an inaccessible flagstick if placed behind the greenside bunker. The trees planted between this and the next hole do, also, seem to have a somewhat magnetic quality.

The advancement of club and ball technology has robbed this tee shot of much of its sting but the area between the medal tee and the trees could easily be shaped to form a tee, increase the hole's length by seven or eight yards and restore the challenge enjoyed by so many over the previous eighty or so years.

Under certain conditions, especially when playing from the front tee, the player can be left with an awkward pitch and run from a downslope to a none too receptive target. The left hand bunker adjacent to the green penalises only the most crooked of approaches, it's banking correcting many more. It would be no great loss to remove this hazard and plant a few, well spaced, Pine trees.

Hole 3   Farl   364 yards   Par 4   S. I. 9

Position off the tee at this hole is important, not so much to set up a good line into the green as to obtain the best lie. Those players unable to hit the ball more than about 180 yards should play slightly left of the marker post giving themselves a flat lie and a good view of their target. The marker, or even left of it, is the best line for the average or long hitter as the contours sweep the ball to the right upon reaching the downslope bringing the gnarled Hawthorn tree at the bottom into play.

The long drive will have a flat stance and only some form of wedge but will lose sight of the putting surface. The drive that gets stuck on the hill will have a view of the green but club choice will be complicated by playing from a downslope.

With bunkers positioned at 12, 7 and 4 o'clock to the green only holes cut in the green's extremities will present any problems to the out of position tee shot.

This hole originally played, in the days before lines of separating trees were planted, to a green close to the present 14th tee. It may well have been the same green site of the original 4th hole. Evidence, in the form of what looks to have been a bunker, can be seen as you leave the present 3rd green.

Hole 4   Harelaw   506 yards   Par 5   S. I. 5

Faced with an intimidating forced carry from the tee, the marker makes a good line for the straight shot. Be warned, however, as any ball straying only slightly right of this line courts disaster. Thick rough, gorse, broom and bracken extends the entire length of this side of the hole. Oh! And so does the out of bounds.

The percentage shot will be played further left and finish in the semi-rough or, for the sophisticated amongst us, played left and an attempt made to move the ball left to right in the air to hold the fairway.

Few will negotiate this hole only on short grass and to complicate matters a shallow bunker threatens the over safe second shot. Just when you think you're home and dry, two steps in front of the green can propel the ball through the back with serious consequences.

This hole is one of the few original Willie Park Jnr. designed holes still in play almost unchanged. The green has been built up at the back, bunkers have been altered or removed but it remains a strong three shotter rarely played without a hindering breeze.

Hole 5   The Covert   174 yards   Par 3   S. I. 15

An impressive short hole where the tee shot is thrown into sharp relief against the backdrop of the mound created from the excavations of the Locher Dam.

Unusually for Old Ranfurly the 5th seems self contained, playing down it's own valley although only a short walk from the 4th green and the 6th tee. Also unusually, the hole's hazards can be seen from the tee. After negotiating cross bunkers there is a distinct advantage in leaving the tee shot short of the hole, thus having an uphill putt, as the green has a more pronounced slope than most. Now in its second reincarnation in the last 10 years this green has gone from a low lying, hidden, badly drained original to today's raised, visible, well drained, uninspired effort. It would seem impossible to make a sloping green dull but that has been achieved here. The intermediate design was poorly constructed but at least had the saving grace of a tier across the middle of the green with subtle variations of slope both above and below. This was deemed too difficult.

Serious trouble awaits the tee shot in the form of deep revetted bunkers which, it has to be said, are completely out of character with the rest of the course, trees almost on the edge of the green and a lateral water hazard all too easy to find on the fly or the bounce. Some of the sting was removed from this area when the out of bounds was moved across the Locher Burn from the nearside.

Hole 6   Carselaverock   502 yards   Par 5   S. I. 13

Probably the hole most likely to yield a birdie and another Park original still played over the same ground. The drive played to the left side of the fairway will be rewarded with a flat lie but will be left with slightly further to go to reach the green as this part of the hole gently curves left to right. Moving the ball round the corner is helped by playing to the centre or right side and letting the contours do their work. Too far right however and, especially in fast conditions, the ball will inevitably end up in semi-rough or, worse, in reeds. The second shot from this side will be complicated by having the ball below the feet and chest high bracken awaits the slice in the summer months. The area just short of the reeds was, for years, a large grass bunker although to call it this is to dignify what was really a large, wet depression. About 25 years ago it was filled and levelled and became known as "Matt's Folly" after the greens convenor of the day.

Generally though, the second shot is untroubled. A large expanse of fairway and semi-rough stretch across the hole and there is little to impede the setting up of the third shot whether this be a pitch or a putt. Not a lot of thought is required. This is a second shot in need of a hazard!

The hole does tighten as you get closer to the green but, really, if you are up to your knees in it here, you deserve it. The green itself appears flattish but has many subtle borrows and, with it being on a similar level to the surrounding area, if you miss the green it is relatively easy to roll three shots into two.

The corrugated nature of this fairway can have a great influence on the playing of the hole best illustrated during an exhibition match in the mid 1970s involving Brian Barnes and Bernard Gallacher against David Huish and David Ingram. All were top exponents of the time. All drives landed within a few yards of each other but three pitched on downslopes and required only mid-irons to reach the green. David Ingram's pitched into an upslope, lost out on any available run and left him struggling to get home with a 3-wood. Now you know why you've never reached this green in two. You're just unlucky!

Hole 7   The Dam   224 yards   Par 3   S. I. 7

This is an excellent par 3 featuring a green set in an area almost surrounded by mounds which wouldn't be out of place on a links course. The player who prefers their golf to be utterly fair will argue that the hole suffers from an unpredictable bounce short of the green but, of course, this works both ways.

A hidden bunker traps many shots played only slightly left of their intended line but many a shot creeps onto the green by missing this hazard on its left side.

Out of bounds, in the shape of the Locher Dam, is sufficiently close to be not only there to visually enhance the hole. The original green site was in the area of today's "winter" green close to the two grass bunkers, and more than a few gutties and Haskells must have sunk without trace.

Recovery from the trees to the right of the green is considerably easier these days since the removal of "Sam's bunker". Named after S.A.Miller who apparently had it installed, it lay on the right side of the green. A small, shallow hazard it none the less impeded any attempt to run the ball onto the green from the long grass which was allowed to grow amongst the trees.

This hole also has a recently twice rebuilt green and is a big improvement on the original surface which was saucer shaped and required a drainage hole at it's centre.

An unfortunate aspect of this hole is that you lose partial sight of your target if you play it at it's full length. Maybe the rear portion of this tee could be built up. Then again, maybe not.

Hole 8   Locherfield   301 yards   Par 4   S. I. 17

We all know of holes where we stand on the tee thinking "birdie" and walk off the green wondering why there is a five being entered on the card. This is one of them! It's fairly innocuous looking from the tee and, given the right conditions, driveable for many.

A good short par 4 will ask questions of every player no matter what their ability and, although more of a penal than a strategic hole, a case can be made for the 8th to fulfil this criterion. Does the longer hitter have the skill and nerve to attempt to drive the green given the severe penalties for failure? Out of bounds lies in wait along the entire length of the hole but really makes its presence felt over the last 100 yards, at times only a dozen or so yards from the direct line to the green. The ambitious player who pulls his tee shot or fails to effect a fade will end up in or behind a copse of densely planted trees with the likely outcome a penalty drop and still no guarantee of a clear view of the green.

The shorter hitter or the player who decides to lay up, would be well advised to be precise for, although only a back, left hole position could be difficult to access, the tee shot that drifts to the right could be hampered by clinging semi-rough and overhanging branches. A single fairway bunker can catch the "not quite laid up enough" shot.

Three greenside bunkers, the back left of which may be superfluous, lie in wait and the over enthusiastic will find trees and even a tannery at the back of the green. Some years ago the leather company demolished a tall chimney which had served as an ideal line for the tee shot. They probably regarded this as progress but there are limits!

As for the green, there is little to be said. For a hole this length, it's dull and unexciting!

Hole 9   Quarry Knowe   426 yards   Par 4   S. I. 1

There are no great secrets to this tough hole. Stand on the tee and it's wysiwyg time although due to the second half of the hole being uphill it plays considerably longer than it's yardage would suggest.

A bunker positioned on the left side of the fairway demands attention from those nervous of the out of bounds but, for the longer hitter, it will only be in play when driving into a strong wind. Left of centre should be the safest and longest line from the tee. Only longer hitters will, for the most part, be able to contemplate reaching the green in regulation and this is not without its perils as the approach is squeezed by trees to the left and long grass to the right.

The stroke index says much about the hole. Anyone receiving a shot and scoring a nett four will win the hole more often than not. Shorter hitters may even have an advantage in that they don't have to make any decisions about their second shot other than hitting it straight and far. Avoid the right side of this hole, "Here be dragons".

Hole 10   Misty Law   382 yards   Par 4   S. I. 8

Not often mentioned as anyone's favourite hole but the 10th is one of the unsung treasures of Old Ranfurly. It is one of the few to have even a nod in the direction of the strategic playing qualities of a dog-leg. On the tee, the decision regarding how much carry can be taken on depends on the player's nerve and ability. Intimidating and frequently into the wind, the drive that keeps to the left side of the fairway will possibly require two clubs less to reach the green than the one that is pushed to the right side. The left of the hole also gives the most open line into the green with an approach from the opposite side having to slide past a bunker that is definitely worth avoiding. The second shot is played against the distant backdrop of Misty Law with even a slight miscue finishing in ever maturing trees on the left or as far as the 11th fairway in the opposite direction. About fifteen years ago a bunker positioned roughly 40 yards short of the green was removed and with it went much of the visual impact of the hole. Reinstated, tweaked a touch to the right, it would have great strategic value.

Two greenside bunkers sit to the left. The front one waits for, and frequently swallows, shots landing just a little short and just a little left. The back one just sits. The green itself is one of the best on the course, rising for a few yards then falling in waves to its low point near the back edge. Any approach shot hoping to nestle close to the flag has to be very precise or get its share of luck as humps and hollows short of the green play funny tricks with the pitch of the ball. How we all laugh!

This hole is now two of Park's originals rolled into one. The first probably played from today's medal tee area to a green in the direction of the 11th tee. The second, the tee for which can still be seen in today's fairway, played to the present green. The green as it is? Today's bunkering? We'll probably never know for sure.

Hole 11　　Auchensale　　482 yards　　Par 5　　S. I. 10

This is a good three shot hole but from the little used "championship" tee it is a very good three shot hole. More of the landing area can be seen from back here and part of the challenge is that if either of the first two shots is even slightly miss-hit the green will still seem a long way off for the approach shot. From this tee the 11th is only about 510 yards, not long by today's standards, but the hole seems to play longer. Why? Well, the drives' landing area has a lush growth of grass which doesn't release the ball and is level along the line of the hole. Thirty yards further on and the landing area is firmer, the grass grows more tightly and the fairway starts to, ever so slightly, run downhill. The second shot encounters an upslope at about 390 yards which few will be able to carry causing the shot to lose more length. All this adds up to a hole physically thirty yards longer but playing sixty. There is a big difference between drive, wood, wedge and drive, wood, 6 iron. In fact it's better than a very good hole!

From the medal tee there is a generous width of fairway but a little thought on positioning can pay dividends. The longer hitter can blast their ball on the direct route down the left side of the fairway and reached a level area safe in the knowledge that he can carry the fairway bunker at 370 yards, possibly even reach the green. Playing to the right side can give extra distance by running off a steep slope.

The player of restricted length encounters more problems. They will not reach a level lie down the left and, on this line, be forced to play a long club with the ball above their feet. Driving to the right side and risking fairway bunkers there, they will have an almost level stance, a view of the green and a line past the other hazards.

This hole has been lengthened over time with the original green, of which no obvious trace exists, being level with the 12th tee. Extensive tree planting in the mid 1990s concentrates the mind where before, vast areas of semi-rough allowed the wayward a great deal more leeway.

Hole 12　　Shillingworth　　415 yards　　Par 4　　S. I. 4

The best way to play this challenging hole, irrespective of ones' ability, is to drive to an area, any area in the right half of the fairway. The right half has everything going for it. It is flatter, giving a bit more length, the semi-rough isn't just as "clingy" and the entrance to the green is more open from this angle. The left side has an upslope, often stopping the drive dead and a bunker 20 yards short of the green comes into play with a vengeance. The second shot has to avoid this bunker, obviously, but from the left the approach that tries to slip past can often get deflected to the right, ending up in a greenside bunker and the approach that carries it lands on firm ground with unpredictable results. From the right the unpredictability is minimised. Finish in a greenside bunker? Come up short? It wasn't the luck of the bounce, you played it that way!

The line from the tee is dead centre of the fairway. This allows the ball to kick and track to the right, hopefully staying on the fairway but it is no great problem if it just goes off. The long driver's biggest problems are the large Birch trees rather than the bunker. A well struck shot, just a bit too far right can easily end up stymied. Neither of the fairway bunkers is particularly deep and given a half decent lie and a half decent technique the ball can be advanced a fair distance.

The green consists mainly of a marked, but playable, slope which varies slightly across the width but with a flat area at the back and a slight ridge close to the front many interesting hole positions are possible. If you're going to miss the green, miss short. Next best, miss right. If you miss left, be in the large bunker. You're almost assured of a good lie. Any further left and you will have to produce a bit of magic coming from below the green, over the bunker and possibly off the next tee. Over club and two small bunkers may stop your ball going out the park. This comes at a price however. Due to the bunkers being only a few feet, front to back, a ball running through the green will almost certainly end up closer to the bunker's back edge, leaving the player with a sloping lie and little room for their backswing. The phrase "only enough room for an angry man and his wedge" would be apt here.

Hole 13   Lawmarnock   121 yards   Par 3   S. I. 18

A short hole that doesn't suffer from a want of sand but it presents these hazards fairly with only a back bunker being hidden from view.

With a hole of this length the distance the player can strike the ball is not really the issue. Indeed the longer club and lower trajectory may well be an advantage as the high shot will be teased and buffeted by the winds to which this hole is especially exposed. The player's ball is either on the green or in serious trouble and finding the ball in the afore mentioned bunker may well bring a sigh of relief as it probably stopped the ball suffering a far worse fate in thick rough, well below the level of the green. No recovery shot ever seems to be straight forward, even from just off the putting surface.

The two bunkers positioned back left are, or at least were at one time, the deepest in the county. (Is that a claim to fame or what?) A back left hole position requires, especially as the green narrows at this point, a shot of great courage, or possibly stupidity, to get close.

It always pays to give downhill putts close attention and on this green more than most. The slopes gradually increase as the putt travels down towards the front of the green and some of the most severe borrows on the course are to be found on the front left quarter.

Hole 14   Tinkers Wood   389 yards   Par 4   S. I. 2

This hole, in common with the succeeding four holes, has always been part of any course layout since 1889. The original tee would appear to have been closer to the gate and the green, although in much the same position, probably more closely followed the natural contours. The position of the original greenside bunkers can still clearly be seen. No less a person than Bobby Locke was apparently well impressed with this hole.

Out of bounds threatens the slicer from tee to green but more so the drive which, aided and abetted by the sloping fairway, can take a hop, skip and jump over the low wall or out the gate if left open.

The unsightly mobile phone mast actually gives the player a good line on this blind tee shot but local knowledge allows the shot to go as far right as "the pink house" before one needs to worry. Playing down the left side may, marginally, shorten the hole but leaves nothing but carry to the green perched on a rough and gorse faced escarpment so shorter hitters should venture a bit further right to leave the possibility of running the ball onto the putting surface.

Missing the green on the left is never a good career move and the over hit approach will get an iffy lie in a narrow bunker or, worse, face a pitch back from the 15th fairway. The green itself is full of problems not the least of which is a slight hogsback which runs along most of its length.

Hole 15   The Ben   321 yards   Par 4   S. I. 14

The tee for this hole was realigned about twenty years ago to point further into the course due to a neighbouring owner complaining about balls in his garden. It formerly aimed the player straight at the flagpole behind the green, which is the direct route but not, perhaps, the best. From the tee the player is confronted with a fairly open expanse of greensward with the anomaly of three bunkers waiting to trap the drive. This is more than any other two or three shot hole on the course.

Longer hitters can disregard the most obvious bunker which should only catch a duck hook but if they choose the direct route two shallow bunkers will ensnare anything slightly pushed or receiving a slight deflection to the right. Even if the ball avoids this fate an outcrop of rough covered rock and a Hawthorn tree lie in wait. The more powerful player also has to choose whether to risk getting caught on the cliff face leading down to the green or even if he wants to pitch from a sloping lie. Laying up left of centre at the top of the hill will present an approach shot from a flat lie to an, almost, discernible target. This same area will be the height of the shorter hitter's ambition and if this distance cannot be achieved anywhere on short grass will do. From only a short distance below the brow of the hill even the flagpole will be out of sight. The distant pylons now come into their own as a reference for lining up. The penalty for over clubbing can be severe, not only in the form of out of bounds but also the possibility of a letter from an insurance company regarding the damage to the car that was minding its own business in the club car park.

The green is probably the trickiest on the course. Hole positions can be found where, even at Old Ranfurly's moderate green speeds, it is verging on the impossible to lay the first putt to tap in distance. Wherever the hole is cut it makes life a lot easier if the ball is played to below the hole. Below and thirty feet away may well be easier than above and six feet. Such is the elevation change, complicating judgement, from the fairway to the green that even members of long standing cannot be sure of where their approach has finished.

In the early 1920s James Braid visited the course, gave recommendations and the club proceeded with the "Braid Scheme". At the time of writing we have no idea exactly what this involved but it did seem to involve holes 15 and 16 at least. For some reason it was abandoned unfinished. Probably some members moaned about it. Nothing's new. Old photographs show a bunkerless 15th green. Are the seven bunkers around the green part of Braid's design? If they were it would be impressive that two of the foremost architects of their day, indeed of all time, left their mark.

Hole 16   The Mound   201 yards   Par 3   S. I. 6

You either love this hole or hate it. There doesn't seem to be an in between. The remarkable thing is that, recently, a book entitled "Britain's 100 Extraordinary Golf Holes" was published and this hole wasn't in it! Makes you wonder what the other holes are like! Uphill pars 3's rarely work, but a blind, uphill par 3? It's only blind once, as the old caddy said. Or, maybe he didn't.

By their very nature one shot holes are of the penal school of architecture, tee, green, one shot to get home but the 16th is as close as it gets for a par 3 to fall into the category of the strategic. Most players assume it their right to reach a par 3 green in one shot and this is where this hole jumps up and bites. A 5 iron and a pitch will result in a four or even a three. A 3 wood may easily result in a five or worse after tangling with the mound. Many a competitor over the last hundred years must have stood on this tee, full of hope and expectation that today's the day that his handicap will tumble and that the monthly medal will be his, only to deposit the remnants of his score card in the bin on the next tee and mutter to himself for the last two holes which he wouldn't even be playing if his partner wasn't trying to score a nett 75.

The principal features of this hole, a cliff face and an ancient earthworks, would be tricky enough to negotiate with a short iron but most will have to play as much as a driver into any wind stronger than a stiff breeze. Rarely does this hole play downwind and then holding the green can be a problem. If the hole is cut on the right side of the green the direct line is over the edge of the ditch surrounding the mound. A safer option would be to aim a bit left and fade the ball. If the hole is on the left side it may be easier to miss the green on the left and attempt to chip and putt. Such is the severity of the slope on this side that it is very easy to run a putt off the green if playing from the middle.

Over the last 30 years this hole has altered quite significantly. The green, now easily the largest on the course, has increased considerably in size, extended to the left over the original greenside bunker and the sloping fringe. The two small mounds to the right mark the area where another bunker once existed and another which sat about 50 yards short of the green caught the over cautious tee shot. Today's hastily constructed bunker is supposed so save the odd shot ending up in the jungle.

Hole 17   Castle Knowe   340 yards   Par 4   S. I. 12

"And now for something completely different". Out of bounds on the left! The Castle enclosure forms this different take on a problem not uncommon on Old Ranfurly. The mature trees and their overhanging branches will also block any pulled or hooked shots that do not have the decency to go out of bounds. If this is the case the only realistic option will be to pitch to the middle of the fairway and try to hole out in as few shots as possible from there. Any shot played too far to the right will fare little better. Large Pine trees being the problem here.

Due to the deep ravine running across this hole many will have no option but to lay up with a 3 wood or long iron. The target area for the tee shot, including that of the player with no realistic hope of reaching the ravine, is a flat expanse between the dip wherein lay the original 1st green and the ravines edge. From there it is a short iron approach. The worst option is to find the ball on the sharply sloping sides of the dip giving the player a variety of awkward stances. It is worthwhile not overclubbing here as gardens await. The ravine can and has been carried from the tee over the years but as the shot has to travel about 290 yards through the air this is not an option for many. Due to the near edge being higher this feature is not immediately obvious from the tee and playing in a pro-am the now Senior

Tour player Bill Longmuir put his drive on the green after his local partners forgot or omitted to inform him of the holes' geography. Or maybe they weren't talking to each other by this time.

The well bunkered green appears fairly flat but has borrows that are not obvious even after prolonged study. Some members subscribe to the theory that more short putts are missed on this green than on any other. Discuss.

The view from the tee is sublime. One can take in parts of the village, Misty Law, northern Renfrewshire and further afield to Ben Lomond and the Arrocher Alps.

Hole 18   Ravine   142 yards   Par 3   S. I. 16

This is obviously not the classical finishing hole. That would be a long, challenging par 4 but with the tee shot having to be played over the ravine to a narrow, ill defined target the golfer has to concentrate to the end. Many rounds have come to grief when all that was required was "one last good shot".

If the green is to be missed, miss on the left as only one bunker lurks and the possibilities for recovery are greater. Two bunkers lie in wait on the right and short-siding yourself here will leave you requiring a minor miracle if the ball is to be laid close. Time was, when running a recovery shot up the banking would have been an option but the present greenkeeping regime dictates the aerial route.

This hole is always intimidating for beginners and the bewildered and a ploy often seen is to cross the ravine at its shortest point i.e. back up the 17th fairway.

In a previous existence this hole played from a still visible tee behind the previous green to the present practice putting green beside the clubhouse. Needless to say the car park did not exist then. It's a better hole now.

The Future for the Course

The land parallel to the fourth hole has been bought at great expense and, in that area, the course boundary secured against any future development. Now all that is required is the small matter of finance to progress any alterations and improvements. The will to do this also has to be there. Change is never welcomed universally. Committees come and go; the membership alters and so do the priorities and wish lists.

The original reasons behind any redevelopment, in no particular order, were to provide worthwhile practise facilities, balance the course (there are three one shot holes in the last six for example), have more of the course playing in a rural setting and that old chestnut, the holy grail of Old Ranfurly, finish at the 15th (many do this already).

The land with selling potential is in the area of the 17th, 18th and few are they who would lament the passing of the 16th. In some ways this would be a pity, they are not the greatest holes in the world but they are possessed of great character. What can be done with the new land? The possibilities are almost limitless. There are no definitive answers in the design of a golf course. If finances allow the clubhouse and its location to be brought into the equation the possibilities expand again.

Change happens naturally over time, teeing grounds are extended in response to play increases, bunkers are maintained and thereby altered (in the last 30 years there has been a nett loss of seven bunkers), ride-on mowers round out the corners of the greens, trees are planted, trees are cut down and so on but when someone comes to write the bi-centenary book they may find that the course has changed every bit as much in its second century as it has in its first.

The Club Champions

To be Club Champion is an aspiration well beyond the thoughts of the overwhelming majority of golf club members.

There is, of course, that largish group of golfer - those having a modicum of talent to their name, who by the law of averages find themselves now and again having half a chance for a bite at the prize…a favourable draw…a lucky break or two when needed…that might be all it takes for them. For most though, it generally ends in tears.

Some of that number though may win the Championship, and occasionally do, during a purple week. Purple week? Every golfer, no matter their handicap has a purple week each year – if they're lucky it might last a fortnight – and that's when everything goes right for them…golf becomes easy…no tinkering with grips or swings…putts drop from ridiculous lengths. And it's useful when this happens during Championship week.

There are a few though…one or two in each generation…who tend to make their mark with distinctive regularity. Strength of character, confidence and composure, all of course linked to technical ability set this group apart from the masses. Psychologists have field days with this lot… and it's not only in golf… they try to find common links between the members of this group. Is it not just that they are simply better at playing the game than the rest of the opposition? Or is that too obvious?

These are the men that have their names engraved on the Old Ranfurly Championship Shield. The only common link between them is a feeling…a feeling that they will all have experienced…that realisation…that they were this year's Champion.

Thomas Fawsitt
(1906 and 1908)

The first Old Ranfurly Champion in 1906 – although he was a bit more fortunate with his 1908 victory as Frank Mingay had a better score (strokeplay) but was disqualified for an error in the treatment of the lost ball rule.

He was an early benefactor of the Club and along with a Mr MacEwan he presented a trophy, played for in the early days, and known as the Fawsitt/MacEwan Cup. The sum of thirty shillings as a prize fund also ensured the thanks of a grateful committee.

He had the impressive sounding handicap of +3 and set a new course record in 1910 with a 73. He was Club Captain in 1911.

Frank H Mingay
(1907, 1909, 1911 and 1914)

Without doubt one of the leading golfers in the area at the time and also one of the most prominent characters in Bridge of Weir. He was a bank clerk but had obvious aspirations in other directions. In 1908 he was granted a U.K. patent for putting incompressible liquids such as: water, treacle, glycerine, castor oil, honey, mercury and frozen liquid pellets into the centre of golf balls. He rationalised that liquid enclosed in the centre of a ball would better receive and transmit club head impact energy at a lower loss of total energy. Liquid core balls had been pioneered by a chap by the name of Jack Jolly but Mingay refined the procedure by the use of injection. The A.G. Spalding Company purchased the rights to his patent and used it to some extent when they introduced the popular 'Witch' in 1916.

Frank Mingay held both the Old Ranfurly and the Ranfurly Castle Championships in 1907. In that same year he took part in a charity match on Christmas Day…along with Messrs Guthrie, Farr and McBean. The losing protagonists (Farr and McBean) being liable for two tons of coal to be distributed among the poor of the village. A sweepstake was organised in relation to the match…with even the winner happily entering into the spirit of the occasion by donating his prize to the coal fund.

Away from golf, Frank Mingay was the Treasurer and one of the leading lights of the Bridge of Weir Tennis Club and was one of those instrumental in getting that organisation off the ground. He was a noted singer in the Church Choir and, perhaps indicative of the character of the man, was first Captain of the 1st Bridge of Weir Company of the Boys' Brigade.

He was Captain of Old Ranfurly in 1913.

Stanley Cohen
(1910)

Stanley Cohen lived in Kilbarchan Rd. Of pleasant demeanour, he was the brother of Harry who was also a prominent member of the club at the time. His family were well regarded in Bridge of Weir - his father, always standing out in the crowd - the stereotypical Jew with the long dark Shylock beard. His Championship victory was remarkable in that he was playing off a handicap at the time of at least 8 shots higher than some of his fellow competitors.

A.B. Ferrie and J.W. Ferrie
(1912) and (1913 and 1919)

Two brothers - who both had the distinction of playing off plus handicaps. As doubles partners they won numerous open competitions.

Matthew Barr Jnr
(1916)

It is very hard to understand why the 1916 Championship was ever allowed to be held. Why it should have been sanctioned by the Club is unknown. Hostilities in Europe were, after all, reaching a peak. Young Barr, however, seems to have come of age during the summer of that year, but in the Championship only had to hold off the challenge of five other rivals to take the honours. He also won the McCulloch Cup in the same year and managed a reduction in handicap from 6 to 3.

James Anderson
(1920)

During the twenties, three different Andersons were to claim the Shield – all unrelated. In 1920, in a field of 19, with rounds of 76 and 74 James Anderson finished three shots ahead of his nearest rival.

John Anderson Jnr
(1921)

In a high scoring, weather affected contest rounds of 75 and 83 were enough to secure victory. In winning the Championship the young Anderson had fulfilled his potential of the previous year when he had lifted the trophy attached to a special stroke competition acknowledging the opening of the extended golf course. He also picked up the J. R. Ross Trophy in 1921.

James Carmichael
(1922)

A former Greenkeeper at Old Ranfurly – he returned from the army and soon reduced his handicap to scratch. In 1921 he was runner-up in an amazing number of competitions, managing to get his name on the Championship Shield the following year.

John Anderson
(1923, 1925, 1929, 1930, 1933)

John Anderson was *the* dominant figure in the affairs of Old Ranfurly, both on and off the course, for more than two decades. Enormously respected – he was mentor and a great influence on all of the McLeod Brothers, among others – his quiet coaching manner guiding rather than pushing. – 'If you don't mind me suggesting,' he would say.

He was often called upon to play in numerous Challenge and Exhibition matches, often against Professional opposition. Among the many credits to his name are that he won the Craigends Cup with A. E. McLeod in 1931 and again with D McMaster in 1933, having the best individual score of the day.

His later victories in the Championship were secured in matchplay rather than strokeplay conditions. He held the Old Ranfurly course record of 67 in 1932 and he was awarded Honorary Membership in 1945.

R Levack
(1924 and 1926)

Bob Levack was quick to make his mark soon after joining Old Ranfurly in 1924. He continued to figure in the prize lists well into the Thirties. He worked for the Glasgow Herald.

John Brodie
(1927 – Shared)

A tall chap, recognisable from a distance by his regular adornment of a pair of brown Harris Tweed Plus Fours, found himself tied with Alastair McLeod after 36 holes of golf. Another 18 holes of strokeplay were called upon and once again they couldn't be separated. As Brodie was leaving the area soon after for a lengthy period, another match was impossible to arrange. McLeod, rather than accept the offered walkover, sportingly agreed that the Championship should be shared.

Alastair E. McLeod
(1927 – Shared, 1931, 1936, 1948)

Alastair McLeod was among the first of those Champions whose golfing careers were destined to be interrupted when the world once again went to war. The first of a significantly talented group who were never really to know what heights they might have achieved. Those pre-war times were undoubtedly the heyday of Scottish amateur golf – numerous personalities, commanding respect and attracting large galleries wherever they played. Alastair McLeod was up there with the best of them.

He came to the wider attention of the Scottish public in 1935 when he secured the Eden Trophy at St Andrews and then went on to defend it the following year.

International honours eluded him until 1937 and even then only after a most amazing performance at the Open Championship at Carnoustie. To read the newspaper reports of the time, one cannot fail to wonder of the impact locally he must have made over the first two qualifying days. The leaderboard read like a Who's Who of World Golf:-

Horton Smith, USA. Gene Sarazen, USA. Sam Snead, USA. Byron Nelson, USA. Walter Hagen, USA. Mr A. E. McLeod, Old Ranfurly.

He wasn't only leading amateur; he was, with Max Faulkner, the leading Briton after shooting a 73 around Burnside followed by an incredible 70 around the Championship course – which remained the amateur course record for many years afterwards. Even though he would eventually fade from the reckoning the eventual winner, Henry Cotton, sought him out and offered him his warmest praise for the achievement.

After being capped against Wales he competed alongside his brother, Walter, in the Home Internationals of 1938, the same year reaching the semi-final of the Scottish Amateur.

The war years failed to dampen his competitive spirit – in 1947, with his brothers Walter and Kenneth, he was part of a victorious triumvirate winning the Western District Team Trophy. In 1948 he won the Victory Cup at St Andrews and crowned his Captaincy at Old Ranfurly by winning their Championship for the fourth time.

He won the championship at Ranfurly Castle twice, the second time in 1952 – twenty-five years after his first triumph at the Old Course.

Alastair McLeod (right) wins the Eden Tournament for the second year in succession in 1936. Here he is seen congratulating the young Dumfries golfer T.E. Donaldson who picked up the handicap trophy. In the centre is the runner-up, George Roberts. Roberts and McLeod had served up one of the most thrilling finals ever in the tournament with golf of an exceptionally high standard. Roberts was perhaps better known nationally as a rugby player. He was Captain of the Watsonians…he was an international cap…being part of the Triple Crown winning team of 1938.

In 1943, Alastair McLeod's brother, Kenneth, was a prisoner of the Japanese building the Burma Railway. In a camp he was passing through he came across a Gordon Highlander in a poorly condition…cerebral malaria. He recognised the young Lieutenant and spent a while at his bed. George Roberts died that evening.

Ian S. McLeod
(1928)

'Coorie' as he was affectionately known, due to his boyhood ability of being able to 'coorie doon low' while sliding on the winter ice, was a popular member of both Bridge of Weir courses and the second of the golfing McLeod brothers. An auctioneer by profession, he was also a prominent local Ice and Field Hockey player. In 1930, with J.R. Hogarth he won the Craigend Cup. A seat to his memory is placed at the third tee at Ranfurly Castle.

Alex MacPherson
(1932 and 1950)

Reading the Champions Board at Old Ranfurly it is noticeable that the winner in 1932 was Alex McPherson and in 1950 there was an Alex MacPherson who took the spoils. It is the same person - a

family decision in the intervening years changed the spelling of the surname.

Alex MacPherson was the eldest, and arguably the best, of three golfing brothers though Jimmy and George were no slouches either. It was Jimmy whom Alex beat in the 1932 final. Jimmy was off plus one, Alex was scratch - the game went to the last green with Jimmy falling victim, much to his annoyance, to the infamous stymie.

In the immediate post war years Alex MacPherson was winning much of what was domestically on offer, shooting consistently low scores including a scratch 65 in 1945.

Walter S. McLeod
(1934, 1938, 1949, 1951, 1952)

You can set your watch by him. Four o' clock most summer afternoons, he drives from his home to the small car park at the fourth tee at Ranfurly Castle. The small adjacent practice area is where he will spend a while. He can get mildly irritated if anyone else has the same idea at the same time. At ninety, one might question his need to practice, 'I go up to practice faults', he says, after all he still has to hold off the weekly challenge at Troon from younger brother Kenneth.

Watch his swing. It's still there, consistent, repetitive, and orthodox. The same swing that won him umpteen tournaments and championships and would no doubt have won him many more if his golfing career, like that of his contemporaries, had not been so rudely interrupted by matters Naval during the early forties.

'I can't hit the ball far enough now', he says, 'and golf is not a pleasurable game if you can't get the ball away.'

But surely Walter, the fact that you can get out and play at all is tremendous?

'This is what people tell me …and then they get annoyed when I keep hitting it straight down the middle.'

The competitive spirit is still very much alive. A spirit honed in the company of his three golfing brothers: 'you didn't want to get beaten by your brother…he would be the last person you'd want to beat you'. A competitive spirit that led him to win the Club Championship at Old Ranfurly on five occasions and at Ranfurly Castle on three, being one of only two players ever to have held both trophies at the same time.

In what has often been described as the golden age of Scottish amateur golf he won most of what was on offer: the Glasgow Amateur Championship, the Tennant Cup, twice, the Renfrewshire Amateur Championship, the Edward Trophy, the Newlands Trophy at Lanark and many more besides. Three times he reached the quarter finals of the Scottish Amateur.

The first time he played for his Country he records as his greatest moment in golf. He was to become the most capped player of his generation in an International career that spanned from 1935 to 1951. He Captained the Scottish team in 1957 and '58.

He had trials for the Walker Cup on three occasions and was a selector in the Sixties.

He joined Royal Troon in 1953 and is now the Honorary President. He is a member of the R&A. He is an Honorary Member of Old Ranfurly. He is the Honorary President of the Renfrewshire Golf Union. The list goes on and on.

 And he wonders: 'how would I have filled in my life if it hadn't been for golf?'

Hugh McMaster

Donald and Hugh McMaster
(1935, 1939) and (1937, 1940)

The McMaster Brothers for a period before the war were providing strong opposition for their McLeod counterparts. In 1933 Donald, in addition to winning the Craigend Trophy with John Anderson, had reached the final of the Eden Trophy at St Andrews and set a new lowest score over Moffat.

Hugh (Taffy) McMaster won the Northern Championship Cup at Lossiemouth in the 1930s and had the pleasant opportunity of burdening Old Ranfurly with the insurance premium to cover the trophy which was valued at £60. He went on to serve as Club Secretary for five years.

Kenneth McLeod
(1946)

Triumph over adversity. In the sporting world it always makes a great story. Don't be confused by tales of sensational comebacks or inspired underdogs upsetting the odds. They are ten a penny.

Real candidates for this category are very rare indeed, perhaps only one or two come along per generation, each achieving a kind of immortalisation as the events of their involvement are passed down to a younger audience. Their stories inspire all sorts of emotional contemplation in the listener.

Go on, name some.

Hogan. Ben Hogan has to be in there for Carnoustie in 1953, winning the Open on his one and only attempt. When his car was hit by the Greyhound Bus…they say that his dive across the passenger seat to save his wife saved his own life too. The engine went through the driver's chair and the steering wheel ended up in the rear. He wasn't meant to walk again, far less play golf.

Matt Busby and the Busby Babes. All but wiped out in the plane crash at Munich and for Matt Busby personally a journey from the door of death in intensive care to the rebuilding of a side that a decade later were to lift the European Cup.

And there is Bob Champion. Few who have watched John Hurt depict him in the movie, Champion, have had a dry eye. From the cancer wards and the chemotherapy to the rebuilding of his strength, did Bob Champion's winning partnership with Aldaniti in the 1981 Grand National not have all the makings of a fairy tale?

And then there's Kenneth McLeod, and a story every bit as inspiring as those others, but a story that has remained local and has been modestly understated for the past sixty years.

In 1946 he won the Club Championship at Old Ranfurly and also the prestigious Eden Tournament at St Andrews which was played in those days to exceptionally large galleries. As an achievement this might be regarded by many as run of the mill especially if you were a McLeod Brother. After all, three of his older brothers had already secured the local title in the past and of those, Alastair, had also taken the Eden in '35 and'36.

The rub here, however, is that only a year earlier Kenneth had just returned to Bridge of Weir from the Far East. He had been a long term 'guest' of the Japanese. He had been helping them build a bridge, a wooden bridge, a bridge that would eventually be immortalised in a movie… 'The Bridge over the River Kwai'.

In the three years of his captivity he contracted numerous different tropical diseases. His legs had been paralysed and a constant exposure to the sun's rays brought skin cancer. For over a thousand days he didn't have a shirt on his back, he wore only a pair of shorts and when they disintegrated he wore a jock-strap made from the remnants of a tent. On his eventual return to Bridge of Weir, his six foot four frame weighed just six stone. He had been one of the lucky ones.

Kenneth McLeod

He had been captured in the jungle of Malaya early in 1942. Kenneth takes up the story himself:-

'I wasn't captured, I escaped…we were set up by a couple of natives…half-caste Chinese…it was market day at Titi…these two young chaps had appeared out of nowhere and said that they would go and get food for us. I was very suspicious…the Japanese came firing at us from two different directions…we were at an apex…there was a stream…one bank was two or three feet high…I jumped it cleanly and got about eighty yards away and went to ground…then there was nothing…just the sound of the crickets…the jungle is never silent…then I heard a voice calling for me, saying that we'd been taken and telling me to go back…I went back…it was my best chance…I had nothing…it was the bayonet in the back and the hands lassoed together.

'We were taken to the police station in Titi, where I was interrogated…they had their swords…and there was a revolver on the table…but I got away with it.

'And we were offered food…tins of food…and the Japanese couldn't read the English labels…so to identify the contents they would stick their swords into the tin so that the juices would run out…and in those days if you didn't eat the contents of a tin straight away you ran the risk of poisoning…and I said to the men, "don't eat that stuff" but some did…they were starving… we buried those men in the lane behind the jail.

'From there, we were taken to the civil jail at Kuala Lumpur and from there we were put into metal cattle trucks, in soaring tropical heat, and transported hundreds of miles up into Thailand. Not all survived the journey.'

The wartime recollections of Kenneth McLeod will always appear to him in vivid colour. Those memories, though, tend to be passed on in only black and white. He spares the listener, only giving an outline, holding the detail. This was a practice he learned in 1945 when visiting the relatives of those soldiers that had been left in the Far East.

Prior to the war, Kenneth had been a schoolboy internationalist but his best golfing years were undoubtedly between '46 and '51. He picked up the Championship at Ranfurly Castle twice in those years also and was, for a number of years, on the verge of further International and Walker Cup honours which were to eventually elude him.

In 1950, he followed up being a semi-finalist at the Scottish Amateur Championship with a marvellous display at the opening event of the West of Scotland Alliance with a superb two under par 69 over Barassie, to finish a full four shots clear of any rival, amateur or professional, with Eric Brown shooting a 73.

Captain of the R&A, Wilbur Muirhead, holds court at the Past Open Champions Dinner at St Andrews on 10th July 1978.

Back Row (L. to R.) – Roberto de Vincenzo, Peter Thomson, Bob Charles, Johnny Miller, Tom Weiskopf, Jack Nicklaus and Bobby Locke.

Front Row (L. to R.) – Max Faulkner, Fred Daly, Tony Jacklin, Henry Cotton, Arnold Palmer, W.M. Muirhead, Tom Watson, Gary Player and Kel Nagle.

Wilbur Muirhead
(1947)

Wilbur Muirhead was good at Captaincies. In fact he made a habit of them. Did someone not say that to be a Captain once is forgivable…to do it twice is just careless? Taking this theory to be correct, Wilbur Muirhead was positively reckless.

He was Captain of Old Ranfurly in 1945. This was his Mother course. He had joined in 1924 as a 14 year old. His father, Arthur, was Captain that year. In years to come he would find himself at the helm of other Clubs: Machrihanish, Western Gailes, the 32 Club and the Shoe Trade Golf Club all made use of his leadership skills and wise counsel.

It was in 1977, however, that he found himself elevated to that highest of all golfing administrations, Captain of the R&A. No one deserved the red dress tails more. He had previously been chairman of the Club's General Committee for three years and of its Championship Committee for four and had been co-chairman of the World Amateur Golf Council. His fellow Past Captains at Old Ranfurly thought it rightly appropriate to honour him with a dinner and reception.

Wilbur Muirhead was a Bridge of Weir man and very much part of the community. A natural shyness sometimes gave an impression of dourness but to those who got close, a thoroughly pleasant and beneficent nature shone through. He was an all round sportsman: curling, junior football, field hockey and ice hockey, where he was capped for both Scotland and Great Britain, were among the many sports he played at a decent level.

Walter McLeod recalls, 'When we were young everyone in the village had two or three sports and Wilbur was no different…the thing about Wilbur, though, was that no matter what team he was in, or what sport he was playing …he would more than likely be Captain'.

Being a Muirhead in Bridge of Weir did, however, carry with it a few extra burdens and responsibilities. The family, through their tannery operation, were the largest employers in the area. With what could be now be classed as a social responsibility that was many years ahead of its time, they encouraged and indeed participated alongside their employees in a wide range of sporting pursuits. They would quietly put in place the facilities, both financial and material, for sport to flourish in the area.

As a golfer, Wilbur Muirhead could have been described as being in the extremely useful category. It was perhaps to his own misfortune that he played at a time when Scottish Amateur Golf was booming with talent. In another age he would undoubtedly have won much more. Nevertheless, he still managed to secure the Championship at Old Ranfurly and during the early fifties he was part of a formidable pairing with L.G. Taylor of Ranfurly Castle.

He played in nineteen successive Amateur Championships where one year at Royal Porthcawl he reached the last sixteen before going down narrowly to the American Champion, Sam Urzetta. Wilbur Muirhead was indeed no stranger to the American style of golf. He held memberships at both Pine Valley and the Augusta National, home of the Masters.

John Arnott
(1953)

It goes without fear of contradiction to say that no one knows the golf courses of Ranfurly, the Old Course or the Castle, like John Arnott. He served as Head Greenkeeper at both places over the years and was indeed himself a golfer of no mean ability.

One extremely common characteristic amongst this listing of Champions is the number of times people will say that they were great putters. The opposite is the case for Arnott. 'One of the greatest golfers I've ever seen,' they will say, 'Pity he couldnae putt…he would have won everything.'

The secret of John Arnott's golfing success was perhaps recently revealed by his boyhood pal, Johnny Coia: 'We had great practice facilities…the front room of John's mother's house in Windsor Place. We'd push up the window and try and hit balls out it and across the railway…we wore a bit of the carpet away…and we smashed a few light bulbs as well.'

Nowadays, the bronze metallic bracelet that Arnott wears is evidence of the arthritic condition that cut short his golf playing career. It will never be, though, the playing of golf that he will be remembered for. It will always be his association with the land, an association spread over six decades. Six decades spent teasing the weather to work for him - learning the timings - and bringing the courses to their peak time and time again. The golfers of Bridge of Weir, then and now, have a lot to thank him for.

Leslie McClue
(1954, 1955, 1956, 1957, 1958)

A maverick, a hustler, a gambler, an oddbod, a chancer, a wide boy, a lovable rogue and just perhaps one of the greatest golfers ever to play at Old Ranfurly. Just a few of the descriptions offered when you mention the name of Leslie McClue.

A somewhat chequered business career, combined with a sometimes flamboyant personal life only adds to the folklore surrounding this most colourful of characters. Those that knew him either loved him or hated him. There seems to have been no in between.

This diminutive, 5ft 6ins, curly haired Renfrew man who walked with a definite limp derived from a childhood illness certainly made Old Ranfurly his own during the late fifties. The only mystery, then as now, is why the International Caps failed to materialise.

It will never be, however, any listing of trophies won that characterises the life of Leslie McClue. Everyone has a story about him, stories in which he always emerges in a sort of 'Flashmanesque' style. These stories, over the years, have been suitably embellished and rounded for maximum effect.

In the 1957 Amateur Championship at Formby Golf Club, Lancashire, he had already beaten the former British Walker Cup Captain, A. A. Duncan, in the third round and had gone forward to meet former US Walker Cup man, Dole Morey.

McClue was 2 up after ten. As they were walking over the eleventh tee Morey stopped to have a practice swing. McClue stood back and thinking he was finished walked forward, right into the head of Morey's driver as he brought it back once again. He was knocked out for almost thirty minutes but, dazed and blood stained, insisted on finishing the match which, amazingly, he went on to win.

It was necessary for him to have nine stitches put in a wound to his ear. McClue pleaded with the doctor not to do anything that might prevent him from playing the following day, so the stitching was done without anaesthetic. Later that evening McClue collapsed. The doctor was so anxious about his condition that he and his wife sat all night beside his bed where, after a most restless sleep, he emerged the following morning to announce that after breakfast he would be on his way to the course for his next match. He was to go down that day, in a gallant performance, 6 and 5 over 36 holes to H. B. Ridgley who would eventually lose in the final to another Scotsman, Reid Jack.

Reid Jack was a friend of McClue's and when McClue moved to live in England and play his golf at the prestigious Sunningdale Golf Club he invited Jack for a game.

'I've arranged a match with a couple of Yanks,' announced McClue. On arrival at the first tee he confirmed with the Americans that it would be, 'the usual five a corner'. It was about the third hole when Reid Jack realised that they were playing for five hundred pound a head, a lot of money in the 1950s. 'I don't have that kind of cash,' he quietly screamed at his partner in a fit of panic.

'Don't worry,' said McClue in steady reassurance, 'this is in the bag.'

And it was.

Leslie McClue was a Professional Gambler. There was roulette and there were horses but it was golf where he gambled most and the money was nearly always placed on himself. Conservative estimates by friends reckon, at his peak, he must have been earning between fifteen and twenty thousand pounds a year hustling on the golf course.

He was playing at Sunningdale one day in terrible weather with a senior member of the Club, Charles Abraham, who was about twice his age. By the time they had reached the eighth green, McClue had claimed casual water on just about every previous one and somehow had mysteriously managed to find that the nearest point of relief had nearly always provided him with a straight uphill putt. The normally mild mannered Mr Abraham could take no more and without any further adieu or warning proceeded to land a punch right on McClue's chin, which knocked him unconscious and left him lying in the middle of the putting surface. When McClue related the story to a friend later in the warmth of the clubhouse, the friend asked him how he had responded. 'I didn't,' said McClue. 'If I'd known that,' said his pal, 'I'd have knocked you out years ago.'

Mr John Churchill, the present Captain of Sunningdale, recalls a celebrated moment when Leslie McClue was making his way home from their Golf Club in the early hours of the morning.

'He fell asleep at the wheel of his Ford Mustang and it careered over a roundabout on the Bath Road and, with all its lights blazing, flew over the top of another car and into the undergrowth. McClue crawled from the wreckage unhurt, but the other driver stopped at a call box and reported a plane crash, as the accident had been on the flight path for Heathrow Airport.'

Leslie McClue died in the spring of 1988 after suffering fatal head injuries during a fall at home. Without question the man had his faults. But is it not a terrific way to be remembered, that whenever someone mentions your surname someone else always smiles and shakes their head with affection?

A.G. Clark
(1959 and 1960)

Sandy Clark is best described in the words of Ian Brodie.

'He is quiet and unassuming and has a wonderful dry sense of humour. On the golf course he was Mister Consistency. He could play with the same ball for three months without losing it. He could go out every time and shoot eighteen fours... but that's not going to win you much. The two of us together in a fourball, however, and we were unbeatable. I got the birdies and Sandy steadied the ship. We had a regular match every Sunday night against Hamish Munro and Stuart McLeod from the Castle...one week at the Old Course and then the following week across the road. It was always £1 on the game and 5/- for individual birdies...that was a lot of money for us at that time. Those were great days.'

Ian Brodie
(1961 and 1966)

He was a wild child of the Sixties. Ian Brodie won the Championship in 1961 he then went to work in London and in Paris. He hardly lifted a golf club for the next five years. Before he could compete in the 1966 Championship he had to visit the Pawn Shop to pick up his clubs. After the victory, over Tommy Houston, the clubs were pawned once again.

'I was skint, we were all skint, this was the swinging Sixties and we were living it up. They offered me twenty five quid for my clubs and I thought that sounds good.'

He had a temper. He was volatile on the golf course. He says that the Locher Dam is full of his putters. He was a scratch golfer yet rarely managed to ever put two scores together.

'I was your classic 69–82 man. I hardly ever won any strokeplay competitions, I could shoot six birdies and still not break 80. Matchplay was my game; I was in at the start of the Newton Shield and generally played number one. I was in the Renfrewshire County Team where you were regularly up against Walker Cup guys, I just loved that. But more often that not I would be out playing golf for money, serious money. There was no other reason to be there.'

Brodie learned his game, like many of his generation in Bridge of Weir, on the Thistle Course. With its ravines, its sow's back and its heavy rough it was an intimidating course for a schoolboy whose main objective was not to lose a ball.

'If you lost a ball in the rough you stayed in the rough till you found another one. This generation don't understand that. You couldn't ask your parents for money for golf balls, they cost more than you got for pocket money. That was our Saturday and Sunday night entertainment…looking for golf balls, a whole crowd of boys in a line shuffling through the rough…it was like a bloody murder enquiry. Then after, we would put all the balls together and take turns in selecting the ones that we wanted.'

His memories of Old Ranfurly flood back. Small bizarre recollections pepper the conversation. *'I remember hitting a drive from the back tee at the second. It was a belter. And then suddenly, Crack! The ball, whilst in mid air, collided with another being played from the third…it was never to be seen again. And once while playing in the McLeod Cup and standing on the sixteenth tee needing a par finish for a really decent score. Wallop! I hit the flagpole on the mound flush on. That was my line in. Predictably, that ball was never seen again either.'*

Ian Brodie hasn't played golf competitively now for some thirty-five years. He still buys golf magazines and follows the tours on television. If he lifted a golf club today everything would soon fall back into place. One gets the impression he just might be too scared to try.

T.C Houston
(1962, 1963, 1972, 1973, 1977, 1981)

Not many people have had a hole in one in a Club Championship final. Tommy Houston has had two. One at the Seventh against Alan Sutherland but perhaps more dramatic was the one he had at the Thirteenth against Alistair Quigg which was to win the match. What a way to close the game.

Tommy Houston learned his game at Old Ranfurly as a boy and to this day is still appreciative of the early support he received from the Club.

'There were a few of us in the Club at that time, I think George Blair was one, who when returning from our National Service were really glad that the then Committee thought fit to waive our admission fees. I think the expression that was used was "that we showed promise".'

T.C. Houston
Six times Club
Champion

And T.C. Houston certainly fulfilled that early promise. Six times Club Champion over the longest extended period of any other winner… nineteen years between the first and last victory. His would always be the first name on the sheet for any Newton Shield match. His contemporaries, still to this day, say what a marvellous golfer he was…but not before they say what a gentleman he is.

However, that modest, almost shy demeanour has always concealed an extremely hard competitive spirit. He won a vast array of thirty-six hole tournaments throughout the country and he picked up the Renfrewshire County Strokeplay Championship at Erskine in 1972.

He now lives in Milngavie and plays his golf at Balmore. He is an Honorary Life Member at Old Ranfurly.

John Houston
(1964)

Doctor John was without doubt one of the most loved characters ever to have graced the links of Ranfurly.

'A damn good golfer...and an even better judge of a glass of whisky,' as quoted by more than one person kind of sums him up.

With his partner in crime, Dan Campbell, he formed an incredibly strong doubles partnership and was a regular player in the West of Scotland Alliance. On one occasion they were returning from an Alliance tournament at Hilton Park, where Campbell had been successful and much alcohol had been taken in celebration. The chosen route home was somehow via the Govan Ferry where, after the crossing, they found themselves in a major traffic jam as Rangers were playing a European tie at Ibrox that evening. With his patience having worn thin the Doc says to hell...pulls the car out and starts overtaking the long line of traffic on the wrong side of the road. A flashing blue light is soon behind him. He stops his vehicle, jumps out and runs back to have a word with the police...he is soon back in the car. The blue lights overtake him and he follows them at speed. Campbell eyes him suspiciously. The Doc looks at him, 'You are Professor Campbell from the Southern General. I have a seriously ill patient at the Thorn Hospital. We have a police escort. By the way, your case is in the back'.

W. C. Smith
(1965)

One of that select band who have been both Captain and Champion. Bill Smith was delightful company. Tall, slim and upright with a pencil moustache, this school headteacher could captivate an audience with conversation of wit and substance. He was a lifetime sportsman. In his younger days he was a junior footballer of some notable ability. In latter years there was disappointment each time he failed to shoot less than his age on the golf course.

Alistair Quigg
(1967, 1969)

People always say the same about Alistair Quigg – he was a class golfer and a very straight hitter. He was also noted for his sartorial elegance on the golf course. An ever present in the Newton Shield Team he was part of the winning side of 1967. He was also a regular participant in thirty-six hole events throughout the Country and would enter the Open Championship at the qualifying stage each year.

Three Past Champions of Old Ranfurly; Dan Campbell, George Blair and Bill Smith who teamed up with Wishaw Professional, Lew Taylor in the Three Plus One, Scottish Sunday Express Pro Am at Cawdor in 1965. One of the first competitions of its kind.

L. W. T. Martin (l) presents Ronnie Kerr with the Championship Shield

Ronnie Kerr
(1968, 1971, 1976, 1978)

You mention the name Ronnie Kerr and the first thing people say is that he was a great putter. He had a mallet headed, hickory shafted weapon that he would use on occasion to devastating effect. In his 1976 final against Bob Mitchell he was in quite awesome form. Mitchell who, off a handicap of seven, had done remarkably well to fight his way through the competition could only stand back in bemusement. Kerr's opening figures for the first round were… 3 4 4   4 4 4   3 3 4   3 3 3 3 – seven under par for thirteen holes. Quite amazing golf!

Ronnie Kerr was one of those late developers in the game and for well over a decade was a dominant force at Old Ranfurly.

George Blair
(1970)

According to Tommy Houston, wee Geordie Blair was a 'Jack Russell terrier of a golfer'…never easy to defeat in matchplay…always ready to bite…especially around the greens.

Being small, stocky and mildly rotund the politically correct way to describe his physique today would be to say that he had a low centre of gravity…somewhat cast in the Ian Woosnam mould. Common with many of his stature there was an ability to hit a golf ball hard and with control. When all parts of his game were firing he was one very formidable opponent. He has played at Old Ranfurly since boyhood

Dan Campbell
(1974)

George Edgar had a putt of no more than four feet on the last green to win the match. Dan Campbell had his cap off waiting to shake his hand. The putt missed. Back up the first. A drive, a three wood and a single putt was what it took. What a time to birdie the first.

Campbell has always been a match player before a stroke player. No one is better versed in the psychology of head to head golf. As an enthusiastic Captain of the Newton Shield team he would have no hesitation in fielding sacrificial lambs at number one if it meant picking up points further down the line.

At the age of eighty, he still plays golf three or four times a week. He refuses to play in any sort of Senior's Competition in case he gets drawn with some old doter (usually ten years younger than himself) who might test his lack of patience. Instead, he is often found with the young. They milk his enthusiasm, savour his company and more often than not pay out their ten pence a hole at the end of it.

A few years ago his golfing career looked all but over. Years of jumping off the back of a moving lorry as an army physical training instructor had eventually taken its toll. He had a golf buggy, a restricted swing and a waning enjoyment. A new hip was required. In stepped fellow Old Ranfurly member, and the best orthopaedic surgeon in the parish, Gerry McGarrity. The buggy has been retired, the bag is carried, and the follow throughs once again finish where they should. He shoots his age on a regular basis.

He is also a dreadful optimist as regards the weather. He can spot the slightest hint of blue in the greyest of skies. He will drag out lesser mortals in dreadful conditions. In the winter he restricts himself to five clubs. When it snows he just takes the one.

He was Club Captain in 1960. He is also a member of Ranfurly Castle and at Shiskine, Arran.

George T. Edgar
(1975)

With him hitting the crossbar the previous year there was never a more popular winner of the Old Ranfurly Championship than George Edgar. A late starter in the world of golf, it has never become clear if his number of golfing trophies ever did manage to exceed the number for badminton. He was tall and back-slapping, sometimes outrageous. The widest of smiles was his trademark. Was there anyone that he didn't wave to on the golf course? And yet beneath all the joviality there lay one steely competitor. He was capable of beating the best – and often did.

George and Alan Edgar

Graeme Conn
(1979)

It was a repeat of the 1978 final - Ronnie Kerr against Graeme Conn – Kerr looking for his fifth victory, the young medical student, Conn, once again looking for his first. It might have been that Kerr had just recently recovered from a hernia operation. It might have been that for once his ultra consistent putting stroke was to let him down. It was much more likely that it was the daily honing of a golf stroke over the long summer break that happened to swing it in Conn's direction. The following year he would go down to an up and coming Alan Hunter in a brave attempt to defend his title. Nevertheless, for Graeme Conn it was three finals in three years. And then the student days were over.

Allan M. Hunter
(1980, 1987 and 1989)

The lowest score ever recorded at Old Ranfurly is 62 by that 'most natural' of golfers, Allan Hunter, in August 1982. It is classed on today's scorecard, somewhat pedantically, as the Medal Course Record as opposed to the Championship Course Record or the Professional Course Record where a few extra yards are played at the fifth and eleventh holes.

Of the round of 31 out and 31 home Allan remembers very little,

'I was playing with Alan McGinley and I just remember being relaxed all day and that despite shooting a new course record I only won the competition that day by one shot. I also remember on the following day, Sunday, I was still on a high and went round in 63 in a friendly game hitting two flagsticks with second shots during the round.'

Another low score, a scratch 64, was to follow and that was to earn him a headline, not to mention six golf balls, in the famous Sunday Express Competition, 'Keep a Six off your Card'. The highlights of that round being an albatross two at the sixth and a birdie two at the sixteenth, an unlikely brace indeed.

It was all happening for Allan Hunter in 1982. Despite losing to the up and coming Steven Thompson in the final of the Club Championship, where he had been 3 up at one stage, he went on to win the Renfrewshire Stroke-Play Championship at Renfrew following on from his County Youth Championship success two years previously.

He certainly took the Stroke-Play Championship in style winning by a margin of six shots from his nearest rival, in a field containing the likes of Scottish Internationalist Barclay Howard and ex-Walker Cup player Gordon Murray. This was despite playing a wrong ball at the fifteenth hole of the second round and running up a seven.

Success in that event catapulted him into the Renfrewshire County Team. Where, alongside Barclay Howard and Bobby Blackwood of Cochrane Castle; Paul Davis of Ranfurly Castle; Paul McKellar of East Renfrewshire and Steve McAllister of Elderslie, they went on to win the Scottish Team Area Championship.

Allan left the area shortly after his third Championship win to live and work in Nottinghamshire. He now plays his golf at Wollaton Park where he has also won their Championship three times.

Steven D. Thompson
(1982)

There are numerous pros and cons for any child whose parents are employed within the licensed trade. When, however, those parents are committed Golf Clubmasters then for a lot of young lads the pros might just distinctly outnumber the cons.

Being brought up on a golf course does have obvious advantages when it comes to mastering the game at an early age.

Steven Thompson was to first pick up a golf club at the scenic Portstewart Golf Club in Northern Ireland. When the family moved to Stranraer his game was such that he managed to take their Junior Championship. When they came to Old Ranfurly his talent immediately caught the eye.

His Club Championship win in 1982 came against a very much in form Allan Hunter, who had collected most of what Renfrewshire had to offer that year. Hunter was three up after just the first ten holes. However, a terrific front nine of 35 in the second round put Thompson in the driving seat and it was all over by the fifteenth.

For the last twenty years, the incredibly modest Thompson has played his golf professionally... with sporadic and moderate success. He topped the Tartan Tour Order of Merit in 1995 and in the same year won the Scottish Professional Match Play Championship. He has featured prominently in Pro-Am events around Scotland picking off prize money and course records on a regular basis.

In 1988 and 89 he qualified for the European Tour, an expensive experience, which by his own admission left him well out of pocket and deeply in debt. Problems with his management company and the liquidation of a major sponsor had not helped the situation. It took a year or two until a level footing was once again reached.

His relationship and connection with Old Ranfurly over the years is difficult to analyse. It would never appear to have been a comfortable partnership. Thompson has continually offered his excellent coaching services to the Club's membership but has perhaps, through his natural shyness, failed to sell himself enough in this capacity. In turn, the Club could never be accused of going out of their way in any attempt to further his career. At an A.G.M. in the late eighties, a member stood up and announced that there was a young man within the Club who was about to seek his fortune on the European Tour and he would like to be given the opportunity of attempting to raise from within the membership some degree of sponsorship that might be of assistance to him. The Board, in their wisdom, wished the Member every success in his endeavours but intimated, somewhat astonishingly, that the Club noticeboard would not be available to him. It does have to be said that this probably did not necessarily indicate any personal slight against Thompson but would, more than likely, have been the response no matter who was concerned.

Of his future there is vagueness. He could turn his attention to full time teaching. He may well be on the look out for an accommodating Club position. However, one gets the impression that the Titleist sponsored Thompson, even though he is now in his forties, feels that there are enough good scores left in him for him to once again feature at a higher level and one day have his walk in the sun.

No matter what he decides to do there are certain things that you just can't take away from someone who has shared the tee with the likes of Ballesteros, Montgomerie, Faldo and Singh.

J. K. Gardner
(1983)

He had the week of his life. Everything went for him. It ended up an all junior final - the youngest final ever - an all Kilbarchan final against Stuart Murphy. Things were very tight until Jim Gardner played the opening nine holes of the second round in only thirty-three strokes. There was no way back for Murphy.

Kenny Morrison
(1984, 1990)

Winner of the Club Championship twice, he has been runner-up on another four occasions. Always a leading contender for the scratch prize in every Club Competition you'll find his name inscribed on just about every trophy in the cabinet.

And he is certainly the man to be playing with if it's holes in one that you are after. He's had five himself but if you want to add in the number that he has witnessed while playing or spectating over the years that figure leaps remarkably to about three dozen!!!

A few years ago he furthered his interest in golf course design by becoming a Graduate of the British Institute of Golf Course Architecture.

Very few have contributed as much time and energy for the good of Old Ranfurly as Kenny Morrison…eighteen years on various Committees…nine as Greens Convenor. No one knows their way round the Course like him either. So who better was there to write in this book a guide on how to play the place?

William Young
(1985)

Willie Young had been a junior member of Old Ranfurly but left it until his mid forties to decide to win the Championship. An all round sportsman, he was a former professional footballer with Renfrew Juniors and Glasgow Rangers. According to his friends (they refused to give their names) he can be somewhat irritatingly deliberate on the golf course with a most ritualistic set up before shots. In the '85 final, against T.C. Houston, nobody gave Young a chance. The general thought was that he had played above himself in just getting to that stage. When it came to finals' day he continued to play above himself. He is now playing most of his golf at Pollok.

Alan H. Edgar
(1986)

His 1986 victory over Kenny Morrison made it a unique double for the Edgar family with Alan taking the title that his father had held eleven years previously. His was a natural talent. He had been Junior Champion the year before and his potential in the game was immense – a potential that still to this day remains untapped. Work commitments currently leave little time for serious golf. What is clearly obvious to those who know him is that while he has undoubtedly inherited his father's charm and personality he has similarly derived his competitive spirit. As far as winning more golfing trophies are concerned… it's now really more a question of when rather than if.

Allan M. Hunter

Kenny Morrison

Steven D. Thompson

A.W. Kidd
(1988)

Archie Kidd secured the club Championship in 1988 against Murray Sharp. Seventeen years later he is still looking to follow up that success with a repeat performance. Only a fool would bet against it happening. At fifty-one, his handicap has been cut to two and he is playing the best golf of his life. He has that dreadfully annoying affliction of making the game look easy. An attacking putting stroke is the strongest part. Putts fall from a distance with irritating regularity. He hates to pay out money on the golf course. He rarely has to.

Hugh MacDonald
(1991, 1992, 1993, 1994, 1995, 1996, 1997, 1998, 2000)

Perhaps the most remarkable thing about Hugh MacDonald, Old Ranfurly's most prolific Club Champion, is that he didn't even lift a golf club until he was twenty-two. He was a snooker player, touring the country, playing in the leading amateur events. In fact, it was two snooker buddies who took him along to Paisley's Barshaw Park and introduced him to the game.

'I just hit the ball as hard as I could', says Hugh.

'They gave me an initial handicap of 12. In those days at Barshaw to get a handicap you didn't have to submit three cards or anything, my pals just told the handicap convenor that I could hit the ball for miles and he was to give me a low handicap, and that was that.'

Shortly he was to join Old Ranfurly. His handicap tumbled and within four years the stocky martial arts exponent was winning the first of his nine Championships.

'When I came to Old Ranfurly at first I played quite a bit with old Hughie Dickie. He was a character. He taught me a lot about the place. Guys like Kenny Morrison and Archie Kidd were the ones I really looked up to and tried to emulate, so when I started playing against them, and being competitive, that gave me a lot of pleasure. You always knew when you played Kenny it was never going to be easy and to beat him you really had to focus. I remember one final against him…I chipped in at the eleventh and he was over shaking my hand and I'm thinking what's going on…but I had won the match…I had no idea, I had been so engrossed.'

Individual success came in a number of thirty-six hole events but it was as part of Gordon Murray's six man Renfrewshire Golf Union Team that took the Scottish Area Team Championship at Machrihanish in 1996 that Hugh still lists as his proudest moment; 'Just playing in the side with the likes of Barclay Howard was enough for me, but to win the thing was tremendous'.

This was followed, the year after, by victory in the Scottish Mid-Amateur Championship, held at Cawder. This particular tournament, which is basically the Amateur Championship of Scotland for over 25 year olds, takes the form of two rounds stroke play with the leading sixteen qualifying for the matchplay stages.

Part of the prize for winning the Mid-Amateur came in an unexpected invitation to form a two man Scottish team with Sam Cairns, now the Professional at Westerwood, to compete in the Simon Bolivar

Cup in Venezuela. This event was inaugurated by the Venezuelan Golf Federation to provide not only a highly reputable golf event but more particularly to establish bonds between Venezuela and other countries through golf. It is staged in honour of Simon Bolivar, the liberator of Venezuela. At first the cup was intended to include only the Bolivian countries and "Mother" Spain. As the years passed the importance and scope of the biennial competition grew and it now includes most of the golf playing countries of the world. Despite Hugh almost initially jeopardising his participation in the event by hanging up the phone on the chap who called with the invitation – he thought he was the victim of a wind-up - and also suffering from a severe bout of food poisoning whilst in South America, he still classes it as the trip of a lifetime.

He left Old Ranfurly in 2000 to make his home in the North East of England. He then took the decision, albeit once again late in life, to turn Professional and for the past three seasons has been associated with Tyneside Golf Club. He has been playing in the Euro-Pro Tour alongside a multitude of wide eyed youngsters half his age. Hugh is the first to admit that playing on this tour without sponsorship has cost him a lot of money. This, however, has been supplemented by his golf club repair business that he operates from mobile premises. His thoughts currently lie with taking a three year P.G.A. Diploma Course which will allow him teaching qualifications. No matter what the future may hold, his place will always be well and truly etched in the annals of Old Ranfurly.

Alistair Lyle
(1999, 2001, 2004)

His first victory was met with the cynical greeting: 'You only won it because Hugh MacDonald wasn't playing'. How unfortunate! How ridiculous! After all you can only beat the opposition that is placed in front of you. The only answer was to win it again…twice.

In 2001 against Matthew Clark he was two down after four. The weather was dreadful, the ground was soaking. Lyle thought the match should be abandoned. Clark and the referee disagreed. Lyle birdied three of the next four holes and was round in 67 for the morning. A steely determination indeed.

A primary school teacher, Lyle's greatest attribute on the Golf Course according to his contemporaries is his dreadfully impressive short game. He has the putter from heaven. Always down in two from the edge of the green. Score saving in strokeplay and soul destroying in matchplay.

Matthew J. S. Clark
(2002)

A very special talent indeed. Still only in his early twenties and already has the County Matchplay and Strokeplay Championships, both at junior and senior level, under his belt.

The youthful gallus arrogance that made you smile has been replaced by a confident respectful courtesy. The slight frame has now expanded and strength has been developed. The timing is impeccable and the ball flies forever. The Professional ranks would have been within his grasp – lesser talents have tried – but a career in banking now has priority.

Gents and Ladies Champions 2005
Graeme Campbell and Ann McKenzie

A regular in the Renfrewshire County Team: tasting success in the 2005 Scottish Area Team Championship. International honours will not be far away for this plus two handicapper if the form that has brought him a significant number of course records in recent years continues to develop.

Clark J. Taylor
(2003)

The 2003 Championship was always going to be very open. Young Clark Taylor would have been very few people's tick. He had been working in America for the Hilton Group; he played a lot of golf while there. He returned to Scotland with a game unrecognisable to the one he had taken away. He was determined and focussed; he was never out of it until he was out. When he stood on the first tee he could look the opposition straight in the eye and show no fear, a big plus in matchplay. He also showed that his Championship victory was no flash in the pan making the final again the following year.

The Centenary Championships
7th August 2005

The Gent's Championship was forecast as the most open for years. There was no outright favourite. Robin Davidson, formerly of Cochrane Castle and playing for the season at number one in the Newton Shield Team, was an obvious choice. Archie Kidd, perhaps playing the best golf of his career, was another. But it was Graeme Campbell, 'Grimble', who those in the know were suggesting would be there at the end…and they turned out to be right.

His opponent in the final was the consistent Stuart Murphy, his second time there…the first occasion being twenty-two years previously, and how Murphy's hopes were constantly raised and dashed during the first eighteen holes. The timing of Campbell's powerful drives was marginally out, and draws were becoming hooks, but each time he escaped serious trouble and there was always a recovery chance…and recover he always did. Seven birdies in the morning round were enough to put him four up and in a position that he would comfortably hold onto in the afternoon. When the game finished on the 32nd Stuart Murphy was only 2 over par and in Campbell Old Ranfurly had a worthy Centenary Champion.

In the Ladies Final over eighteen holes, a large gallery watched Ann McKenzie take on, and defeat, Shirley McKnight in a contest far tighter than the eventual 6&5 result would suggest.

But it was the Junior Final, however, that captured the imagination. Two brothers, Sam and Jamie Binning, were the protagonists in what turned out to be a thrilling match – although their emotionally battered parents might have other words to describe it.

Fifteen year old, one handicapper, Sam was a pretty sure bet to take the scalp of his six handicapped, younger brother who was playing from the back white championship tees for about the first time. It was generally predicted that over thirty-six holes the more experienced Sam would easily prevail and for thirteen year old Jamie… well he would live to fight another day. Just that no one bothered to tell this to Jamie.

The first eighteen holes were pure exhibition golf. Jamie Binning had the round of his life, a scratch

69. He was five up. But the match was only halfway and back Sam would come. However, despite him cutting the margin to three by the ninth… by the eleventh it was back to five again. Sam then took twelve and thirteen and fourteen was halved. On fifteen, Jamie had a putt, across the slope, to win the match. It went five foot past and it was missed on the way back. The margin was two. Both missed the green at sixteen but it was Sam who got up and down. There was one in it. Jamie had another putt on seventeen to win the match. Once again it went a nervous five foot past. This time he got the return. There was still one in it.

Sam's tee shot at eighteen found the back right bunker. Jamie had to produce just one last sure solid strike… and produce it he did. His ball checked on the centre of the green and it was Goodnight Vienna. The quickest of sporting handshakes was offered. Did Walter McLeod not always say that the last person you wanted to be beaten by was your brother?

And just like the McLeod brothers, who battled against each other on many occasions over Old Ranfurly three generations previously, the Binnings seem also to have that talent for other sports. Sam for cricket and football and Jamie with rugby and basketball. Let us all hope, however, that is with golf that their attention is eventually focussed. This was a truly great final.

The boys were also to face each other in the final of the Boys' Championship at Ranfurly Castle. Sam got his revenge. Honours even.

The Ladies

By the time the Old Course Ranfurly Golf Club came into being a Club exclusively for Ladies had been in existence in the village for nine years. The Bridge of Weir and Ranfurly Ladies Club was in good stead and was, in 1905, ready to move location, from its original home at Horsewood, to an area at Clevans, let to them by the newly situated Ranfurly Castle Golf Club.

It would seem at the time of the formation of Old Ranfurly that there was no demand, or even thought, for the admission of Lady Members. This is not to say that ladies were not welcome, far from it. One of the first duties of the Old Ranfurly Secretary was actually to write to the Ladies Club confirming that they were welcome to hold their mixed foursomes competition over the Old Course.

The first Committee at Old Ranfurly were obviously way ahead of their time in terms of gender equality. The Ladies of the area were soon to be offered the most generous of playing conditions available anywhere. The rules were drawn up with such wonderful chauvinism:-

Bye – Laws
By Directors, containing the
Conditions on which
Ladies
May be <u>allowed to play</u> on Course

Subject to the conditions hereinafter contained, the Committee may allow Ladies to play on the Course on payment in advance of the Subscription Rates after mentioned.

The name of any lady desiring to play for more than one day must (after application in such form as the Committee may from time to time determine) be first approved (a) by a Member of the Club, if the period of play does not exceed a week, (b) by a Member of the Committee, if the period of play be more than one week but does not exceed one month and (c) by the ballot of the Board of Directors, if the period of play be for one year.

The following are the Subscription Rates payable by Ladies until further notice, and these Subscription Rates are payable by all ladies who shall play on the Course, whether by themselves or with Members:-

1 Day _____	**£0.1.0**
1 Week _____	**£0.5.0**
1 Month _____	**£0.15.0**
12 Months _____	**£1.10.0**

Ladies shall only be allowed to play under the following restrictions, and these restrictions shall apply to ladies, whether playing by themselves or with gentlemen:-

(1) They shall not play on Public Holidays, Medal Days or Competition Days.

(2) On Saturdays, where neither Medal nor other Competitions are taking place, they shall not start after 11 a.m.

On any other day on which they are allowed to play they shall not start after 4 p.m.

The hour of starting is liable to alteration from time to time.

(3) They shall not start from the first tee unless there are no Members, Ordinary or Temporary, ready to start.

(4) They must allow Members to pass without being asked to do so.

(5) They shall have no use of the Club House, nor shall they be allowed to introduce visitors to play on the course.

Lady players will be bound to conform to the general Rules of the Club.
The Committee reserve power at any time to suspend or withdraw the privilege of playing granted to Ladies.

The Club House
Bridge of Weir, 12th June 1905

By 1915, there were seventeen ladies listed as having the privilege of the course. Most, if not all, of these ladies were wives or daughters of members of the Club. At this time the Club, like others in the area, was suffering financially and the membership was sorely depleted due to the implications of the Great War. Members were being encouraged to canvas for new blood.

The Committee issued a statement:-

'The Committee consider that Lady Members would be a source of strength to the Club, not only in themselves, but in the probability of their being an inducement to Gentlemen Members to join.'

An inducement indeed!! You can just imagine it. 'I'll away up and join Old Ranfurly, they've got women.'

Anyway, it was unanimously agreed that they be admitted on the following terms.

First – As Associates.

Second – Their numbers be limited to fifty.

Third – Annual Subscriptions 10/6 with 10/6 for current year.

Fourth - The privilege to play any time on week days before 4 p.m.

The privilege to play any time with a Gentleman Member excepting Saturdays and Public Holidays.

The privilege to play on Saturdays after 5 p.m. with a Gentleman Member.

It was, however, desirable that proper accommodation be found for the ladies and the Committee suggested, 'altering the East Room for that purpose and taking in the present cool house.' Alexander, Joiners estimated the cost of the alterations at £14.13.0

By 1919, the Ladies Section had developed within the Club to such an extent that they were now electing their own Captain. They were also obviously gaining the respect of the Gentlemen at the helm, as the Secretary was instructed to write to the Lady Captain informing her that a Permanent Building Committee had been set up, and they would be happy to meet with the ladies to consider any scheme they were prepared to put forward in the interests of the Club.

Recognition indeed.

As the Ladies Section blossomed – they now had a waiting list - they were frustrated to find that they were recognised as officially having no real standing as a Club and that could only be rectified by becoming members of the Ladies Golf Union, the fees being £3-3/- per annum. The Directors instructed the Secretary to pay the said fees, as the Ladies Section had no finances.

In 1927 the Ladies were to have their own Constitution adopted within the Club. This brought, within their ranks, a new found confidence, and their deputations were soon treading a constant path to the Director's meetings. They wanted provided with four comfortable chairs for the Ladies Room - they were told to go and get them but not to spend more than £9. They complained about their fourteenth tee and said they wanted something better - they got a better tee. They complained about having no hot water in their room - the tap was tested and the hot water ran freely. The ladies were surprised. The gentlemen hid their smug expressions well.

In those early days the ladies played a course quite similar to the men. Within living memory they teed off from the bottom of the hill at the fourth, until a certain Green Convenor's wife couldn't get up the hill and it was changed. They also teed up from the bottom of the hill at the sixteenth until it was realised that whoever got up the hill won the medal.

The Ladies Golf Union also had a rule (since rescinded) that forbade a competitor from leaving the course for any reason during a competition. So, while the gentlemen could jump into the Clubhouse to spend a penny while they waited for the sixteenth green to clear, the ladies just had to do a wee dance then get on with the last three holes.

On the playing front, it was not until 1954 that the Ladies played for a Championship Trophy. In fifty-three years of the event it is interesting to note that it has been won on forty-three occasions by one of five ladies. Wilma Aitken has secured it fourteen times. Doris Robertson was the leading light in the fifties and she took it ten times. Marilyn Muir has held it nine times and there is likely more to come. Mary Borland, the secretary of the Ladies Section for umpteen years, showed that she could play a bit too by taking it six times and Rena Anderson won it four times between 1985 and 2000.

As the years have passed, so the ladies involvement in the general running of the Club has increased. In fact we have now, just this year, reached an age of equality. Ladies now pay the same fees as the Gentlemen. They are entitled to the same times on the Course. They have full voting rights and a voice at the A.G.M. No longer does it say in the yearbook that there is no restriction to them playing on winter nights. No longer do they have to worry about stepping off the carpet into a crocodile infested part of the Clubhouse. Some have even been spotted with a pool cue in their hand.

Surely things have gone too far?

Maybe it's about time.

The Start of the Centenary Year

On Friday 21ˢᵗ January 2005, one hundred years to the day since the first recorded meeting of those interested in forming the Old Course Ranfurly Golf Club, the current members along with their families and friends flocked to the clubhouse. No one could remember the place being quite as busy, and with such a wonderful atmosphere of conviviality prevailing. Young anoraked children, who'd heard that there was going to be fireworks, outnumbered the blazers and ties of the large deputation of Past Captains.

Captain George MacDougall gave a brief welcome, introducing a selection of those who had served the club with distinction throughout the years, before heading outside into the freezing air with the centenary flag raising party.

To the sound of Past Captain John Langan's bagpipes, the purple flag rose on the floodlit pole exactly one hundred years to the minute from when that first meeting would have convened. With the short formalities over, the clear perfect sky erupted with pyrotechnics. Audible gasps of delight were heard from the large gallery assembled outside the clubhouse, and not only from the children, as showers of colour lit up the darkness overhead.

In the clubhouse a buffet was provided – a table was laid out with memorabilia – members with glasses in hand drifted from one cheery group to another – the older members held court, regaling the younger ones, that had the good sense to listen, with tales of bygone days – many of which, subtly embellished over the years for entertainment value, possibly still containing the odd vestige of truth.

Inside, in the warmth of the clubhouse, an air of happiness continued throughout the evening. Outside, in the chill of night, the spirits of differently dressed men looked through the windows and nodded to each other with contentment. The centenary year had begun.

The Centenary Ball

On Friday 6th May 2005 over 250 members and guests came together at the Glynhill Hotel, Renfrew and danced the night away in an evening blessed with that perfect level of formality. Captain George MacDougall welcomed his counterparts from Ranfurly Castle and Kilmacolm to his top table along with the Lord Lieutenant of Renfrewshire, Cameron H Parker Esq. O.B.E who ably and wittily proposed the toast to the first 100 years of the Old Course Ranfurly Golf Club.

The guests were piped in by Past Captain John Langan and Mr Sandy Clark assumed the role of Master of Ceremonies for the evening. The two local hospices gained the sum of £2440 from the proceeds of a raffle and an auction.

The Centenary Ball Top Table
from L to R Back: Ken Campbell (Kilmacolm G. C.), Marilyn Muir, George MacDougall (Capt), Cameron H. Parker, Bill Donaldson (Ranfurly Castle G.C.), Mrs B. Clark, John Clark
Front: Mrs S Campbell, Mrs A MacDougall, Mrs M Parker, Mrs E Donaldson

Centenary at Ranfurly Castle

Over the road meantime, the members of Ranfurly Castle were embarking on their own Centenary celebrations, it was after all the one hundredth anniversary of their 'new' golf course.

On the 27th May 2005, exactly one hundred years to the day since the Captain, James Cuthbertson, stood on the first tee and opened the course with a ceremonial drive, the present incumbent to the office, Bill Donaldson, took part in a re-enactment of that honourable tradition. Following an interesting and scene setting introduction by Past Captain Craig Reedie, he stepped forward in front of a very large gallery and, despite a period of enforced posturing as the event was recorded for posterity, he proceeded in hitting a majestic drive well towards the green. His ball was the target for the speediest junior to recover in order to receive a token of the evening.

The formal proceedings over, the protagonists who would join the Captain in a two-hole exhibition match over the first and eighteenth holes were then announced on to the tee. The Captain would be partnered by Kenneth McLeod, 86 years old and senior Past Captain of the Club and former junior internationalist. They would play Leslie Taylor, former internationalist and finalist in the Amateur Championship almost fifty years previously who would be partnered by Walter McLeod, himself many times capped and a winner of more things over the years than you could care to mention.

Bill Donaldson displayed an impressive steadiness of nerve as he hit an identical shot to his previous to get the match started. Next up was Kenneth, resplendent in plus fours, who, with a quick swing, guided a hard and low shot on the perfect line. Leslie Taylor was next. Carrying a few pounds over his normal fighting weight he hit a strong high looping drive landing a few yards from Kenneth's ball, well beyond the distance of the bunkers. Walter was next up. Ninety years old. Modern, expensive looking waterproofs…black shiny glove…cap…his daughter caddying for him…from behind he had the physique of a man a third of his age. The tee went in the ground and he was back up in one motion…no grunts…no aches or pains…he looked at the shot and with a swing of discipline he hit through the ball at speed… and was down picking his peg up as the ball soared on the optimum trajectory to join those of his contemporaries in an impressive grouping.

The faces of those in the gallery were a picture. They had come to humour the old guys. Jolly good show boys, great to see you. Instead there was smiles of disbelief, quietly muttered swear words of respect, and after the applause died down everyone realised that this was going to be worth going up the fairway for.

And worth it, it was. This triumvirate of Past Champions were not there to be patronised. The large respectful gallery brought back memories for each of them… memories of past victories. People were watching them play golf once again… age had nothing to do with it…the visualisation of the shot was the same. The years fell off them and from a dreich night they were back in the sunshine of their youth. Walter McLeod pondered long and hard about his approach…changed clubs…and fired a long iron straight at the pin. The heavy night brought it up short. Kenneth was short and left and was faced with a wedge shot over the shoulder of the protecting bunker. From thirty yards he put it stone dead.

The eighteenth was always going to be a tricky prospect against a strengthening wind. Nevertheless, neither Leslie nor Walter were far short in two, the former then throwing in an exciting high approach right on the pin, the ball having the audacity to pull up short when the backspin checked its second bounce. It would have been a great night for a long putt or two to have dropped but it was not to be. It was pure entertainment. It was sporting handshakes all round. Captain Donaldson had shot 4/4. Nobody cared. He was delighted.

Ninety year old Walter McLeod tees off during Ranfurly Castle's Centenary Celebrations

After the two hole exhibition match to celebrate the centenary at Ranfurly Castle
L to R - Bill Donaldson (Captain), Leslie Taylor, Water McLeod and Kenneth McLeod

The Grand Match

Following on from a very successful Family Day, the Grand Match was the last outdoor occasion on the calendar of centenary celebrations. The weather played its part once again as the country basked in an early September heatwave.

A format was found that was competitive whilst also being extremely sociable. It was four to a team, with most teams comprising of a man and a lady from Old Ranfurly, a guest from Ranfurly Castle and a guest from Kilmacolm. The two best nett scores going on the card.

There was a sense of occasion. For six and a half hours the starter, George Ford, organised the groupings. The dulcet tones of Jim McCafferty called them formally to the tee. There they were met by either Harry McNeil, a Past President of the Renfrewshire Golf Union, or David McDougall. Has there ever been a better servant to Old Ranfurly than David McDougall?

The course was resplendent. The smooth greens were faster than ever. Dave Cunningham from Ranfurly Castle had an albatross two at the fourth; his playing partner Stewart Hunter could only manage an eagle. Playing with Robin Davidson and Mary Lochhead, this wee bit of excitement would help to eventually sneak them into third place.

It was ten holes to Jean Clark at the drinks tent. Ice cold gin and tonic in the summer sun. Let's stay for one more.

A team comprising of the four Captains played some excellent golf to politely finish second but the decanters for first prize went to a side composed of youth and experience. Gordon Airs from Kilmacolm, Derek Gray from Ranfurly Castle together with Alison Moss and Ewan Grimes from the Old Course managed a winning aggregate score of 120.

A hot and cold buffet was laid on. Help yourself to a glass of wine. An atmosphere of conviviality and pride was felt once again as the clubhouse rang with laughter. A happy day's golfing with friends is a great way to celebrate any anniversary.

Past Captains L to R
Back - J. F. Stewart, C. F. Crabbe, A. R. J. Dunlop, G. R. Hepburn, J. H. Langan, S. D. Gibson, W. L. H. Campbell, P. Herbert
Middle - G. L. MacDougall, T. McClure, G. C. Ford, G. M. Smith, F. B. T. Muir, C. M. Gilchrist, W. S. McKenzie, I. Watson, G. S. A. MacDonald, A. M. Connell
Front - E. G. Cummings, J. S. Leckie, D. Campbell, M. U. Sim, W. R. Miller, W. C. Smith, J. C. Smith

The Last Quarter Century

It might have been around the early eighties that Minute Books started to get boring. In saying this I'm not referring directly to the books of Old Ranfurly or any other particular organisation nor am I decrying the good work of any Secretary or Past Secretary. It's just that the electronic typewriter, and latterly the word processor, has undoubtedly stripped historical records of any passion. Without the luxury of a delete key, the emotional hieroglyphics of the early scribe were carved onto the pages of the bound books with an individual personality and style. A bond would then develop between reader and original writer. Beautifully crafted, calligraphically rounded letters and flowing sentences give an indication of balance and appeal. The jagged, tight and angular pen reveals a frustrated impatience. Through the dried ink the dead reach out to touch the living. Today's sanitised, adjective free, strictly business like affairs robs the reader of so much unconscious pleasure.

Perhaps the most interesting points in the Minute Books of recent years, especially if one revels in a degree of voyeuristic schadenfreude, are the noting of the various disciplinary indiscretions that from time to time occur. Being now aware of the pedantic world of 'Golf Committee Justice' it may be quite useful at this stage to issue guidelines, based on Old Ranfurly's Minute Books, as to just what can and cannot be got away with:-

Being drunk in the Clubhouse on a regular basis is not recommended. As well as being obnoxious you are more than likely to eventually tell other obnoxious (but sober) people what you think of them. The problem here is that they will remember the conversation, you won't. The defence case stumbles.

Never cheat on the golf course. Fiddling a lie is akin to child molestation and a ball down the trouser leg is on a par with punching your granny. In a friendly bounce game the over enthusiastic identification of your ball or a muffled shout of rabbit scrape can sometimes achieve a worthwhile result. Any cheating should always be able to be classed as dubiously legitimate.

Stealing golf clubs is not a good idea. It is far better to get a loan of them and then don't give them back.

Air rifles should not be stored within lockers. The rabbits on the course bring us a bond with nature. Any future culling will be put out to tender. The fact that you already have a gun on the premises will not influence the Committee's decision in this matter.

Do not pin amusing things on the Club noticeboard. The drawing pins will be tested for DNA. They will find out that it was you.

Do not approach the Greenkeeper with advice. This practice may be full of good intent but it does seem to be more prevalent when the Course is not perhaps at its best. You will not get the appreciation or recognition that you deserve.

Try not to swear on the Course, even at oneself. Swearing at another member may be tolerated if it can be proved that he is as equally inadequate as yourself and that you have provided at least some degree of entertainment for your playing partners. Swearing at Ladies, however, is a major no-no and will bring out the chivalric tendencies of your erstwhile chauvinistic fellow members. This really requires swiftly dispatched bunches of flowers to neutralise a rapidly deteriorating situation.

Greenkeepers 2005
John Hunter, Iain McKendrick, Ian Morrison (Head), Alexander Hunter, Crawford Stevenson

It is hoped that the above pieces of advice may prove useful. They are all based on real life incidents. Names have been omitted to protect the innocent.

Occasionally, also, the mail brings some relief.

A letter was received from a ship's Captain who was a member of the Old Course saying that as he was at sea for nine months in the year could the Committee see fit to offer him a reduced membership fee. The Committee, in their wisdom, sent him a very polite reply saying that they hoped that his time at home coincided with the golfing season... as he wasn't getting any discount.

Members of Kelburne Hockey Club also received a negative response to their request that four of their members might play a round of golf with hockey sticks rather than golf clubs. It might have been far more entertaining, when you think about it, if they had gone and played hockey with golf clubs.

Suzanne Noble and Stephen Coull

Since 1980 the business side of things at Old Ranfurly could be described as being adequately consolidated. No major building projects have taken place though the monetary figures required in keeping the clubhouse up to scratch would astound the Club's forefathers. On the Course, the purchase of the land at Auchensale, adjacent to the fourth hole, was a major capital outlay and perhaps one day in the future it might be considered to have been value for money. Talks have been ongoing with several interested developers since the mid 1990s over the sale of land to the right of the first hole and including parts of the seventeenth and eighteenth holes. This action does not seem to arouse any great enthusiasm from within the rank and file membership of the Club and one would guess that any offer eventually on the table would have to be so ludicrously over the top before it would have any chance of acceptance.

Bar Staff
Katie Ferris and Jean Clark

On the playing front there have been several individual performances to note, not least the recent fine effort by Neil Stewart in reaching the final of the County Matchplay Championship played over Old Ranfurly in its centenary year.

As regards the Newton Shield team, depth of quality seems to be an issue. Home games are mostly secured, away matches rarely are. This situation seems to be even more in evidence when the Muirhead Trophy is competed for against Ranfurly Castle. It has been a long time since 'Old Ranfurly' has been inscribed on the cigar box.

In Clubmasters there has, until recently, been a degree of stability. Mr and Mrs Derek Thompson arrived in 1980 and remained for a decade. After their retirement came Allan and Liz Shearer who, with Liz front of house and chef Allan in the kitchen, provided a first class service for over thirteen years before moving on to Cochrane Castle. After a couple of unsettled years, with a number of agency chefs and a couple of short term occupants in the Clubmaster's role, Stephen Coull and his partner Suzanne Noble are now providing for the needs of the members and the early signs are, by general consent, most promising indeed.

The administration of the Club has for the past five years been in the capable hands of former I.T. professional, Quintin McClymont. Previous to taking up his office at Old Ranfurly an evaluation of lifestyle had been undertaken by him. Airport departure lounges and impersonal hotels no longer held one iota of attraction. It was all about quality of life and Quintin's previous experience on the Board at Kilmacolm Golf Club made him the ideal candidate for the position at Bridge of Weir.

Ironically, since taking up the position at the Golf Club, the one thing he hardly ever does now is golf. Angling is his sport. The non-competitive, contemplative escapism appeals to his character. It fits his character.

Since 2002, the quiet efficiency of Aileen Wilson, as Admin Assistant, has been greatly appreciated by the Club.

Aileen Wilson and Quintin McClymont

Ian Morrison has been Head Greenkeeper for the past seven years. Having served his time at Renfrew and at Killermont he was in charge at Bramall Park Golf Club, Stockport before coming to Bridge of Weir. He has an air of quiet authority. His focus is clearly on long term improvement and development. He delights by being hands-on... enjoys the winter...the building work...the reconstruction. Understandably he, like so many skilled and expressive tradesmen in numerous types of employment, gets mildly irritated at the ever burdening paperwork of administration. To him there is an attraction, which many would fail to grasp, of working outdoors...figuratively painting and gently changing a landscape...presenting his work like an artist.

But what of the future?

For the past one hundred and sixteen years golf has been played around the links of Ranfurly. The same passage of time again will take us to 2121.

The contemplation of world events that will occur in this time doesn't even bear thinking about. Man's inhumanity to man will continue to make countless thousands mourn. His capacity for self destruction will increase dramatically. Greed and famine and war will remain an issue and the colours in the atlas will change.

But an ancient mound will still stand…an ancient mound still connected, in the dreams of every local schoolboy, to a nearby ruined castle by a secret mystical tunnel. Around it they might still play golf. There will be wayward drives and missed short putts. There will be holes in one and drinks to celebrate. There will be excitement and drama… there will be triumphs and disasters.

And on the last green the players will shake each other's hand.

Nothing will have changed.

Club Captains

1905 John Gray	1940 T A Fairbairn	1973 E G Cummings
1906 John Gray	1941 D A McKay	1974 G M Raeside
1907 John Gray	1942 D A McKay	1975 Walter A Wilson
1908 Harry W Farr	1943 D A McKay	1976 W H O'May
1909 Harry W Farr	1944 Wilbur M Muirhead	1977 Andrew M Connell
1910 Harry W Farr	1945 Wilbur M Muirhead	1978 G S A Macdonald
1911 Thos W Fawsitt	1946 James T Scott	1979 George T Smith
1912 James G Caldwell	1947 Charles Shirreffs	1980 Ian Watson
1913 F H Mingay	1948 Alastair E McLeod	1981 Charles J McGinlay
1914 James H McGee	1949 R C Graham	1982 J B Wilson
1915 Francis D Brown	1950 R K Garner	1983 W S McKenzie
1916 Francis D Brown	1951 A N Macfie	1984 Crawford M Gilchrist
1917 Francis D Brown	1952 Mathew U Sim	1985 Finlay B T Muir
1918 George Hector	1953 Sam Miller	1986 George M Smith
1919 J B McKinlay	1954 Alec E Smith	1987 G C Ford
1920 James Barr	1955 A P Paton	1988 E W Smith O.B.E
1921 James Barr	1956 John P Holmes	1989 James F Stewart
1922 R Finlay Harvey	1957 John Hall	1990 Thos McClure
1923 Dr A D McLachlan	1958 John S Judge	1991 G L MacDougall
1924 Arthur M Muirhead	1959 William C Smith	1992 C F Crabbe
1925 John E Highton	1960 Dan Campbell	1993 A R J Dunlop
1926 Thomas J Hill	1961 J A Gibson	1994 G R Hepburn
1927 Albert J Hendrie	1962 Andrew Wilson	1995 J H Langan
1928 Archibald Miller	1963 J C Smith	1996 Stuart D Gibson
1929 Walter C S McGlashan	1964 A B Kerr	1997 W L H Campbell
1930 J Victor Cunningham	1965 J Stevenson	1998 Peter F Herbert
1931 John Ireland	1966 John Houston	1999 W R Miller
1932 A McMaster	1967 D M Gibson	2000 Robert Murdoch
1933 James W Nelson	1968 L W T Martin	2001 Gary G Cruikshank
1934 A G Brander	1969 G W Blyth	2002 Peter F Herbert
1935 D MacCulloch	1970 J Ross	2003 W R Miller
1936 John Anderson	1971 John S Leckie	2004 Andrew G Gardner
1937 George A Davie	1972 J C Osborne	2005 G L MacDougall
1938 W Loudfoot		
1939 William P Sproul		

Lady Captains

1919	Miss Anne Caldwell	1953	Miss Jane D. Russell	1980	Mrs I Watson
1920	Mrs Mary Barr	1954	Miss C Marshall	1981	Mrs R Aitken
1921	Mrs Mary Barr	1955	Mrs Marion H Tallersall	1982	Mrs M Fleming
1922	Mrs Dais Fergus	1956	Miss Parkin /	1983	Miss E.J.C. Caldwell
1923	Miss Isa M Telfer		Mrs Hilda I Judge	1984	Mrs I.C. Robin
1924	Miss Isa M Telfer	1957	Mrs Hilda I Judge	1985	Mrs B.D. Stewart
1925	Mrs Anne G Mackie	1958	Mrs J Robertson	1986	Mrs A Hillcott
1926	Mrs Anne G Mackie	1959	Miss Mary R R Borland	1987	Mrs M.F. Mitchell
1927	Mrs Isa M Telfer	1960	Mrs G Ham	1988	Mrs M.J. Dunlop
1928	Miss Cecilia M Weir	1961	Miss I.H. Kennedy	1989	Mrs J.L.G. Wooler
1929	Miss Cecilia M Weir	1962	Mrs T Taylor	1990	Mrs R.A. Lavety
1930	Miss M M Hector	1963	Mrs J.M. Simpson	1991	Mrs G Rintoul
1931	Mrs Andrews	1964	Miss M Malcolm	1992	Mrs M McKnight
1932	Mrs Andrews	1965	Mrs J.F. Woods	1993	Mrs V Cummings
1933	Mrs J R Miller	1966	Mrs Wm C Smith	1994	Mrs E.O. Bayne
1934	Mrs J R Miller	1967	Mrs Stewart Kerr	1995	Mrs M Herbert
1935	Miss Peacock	1968	Mrs G.T. White	1996	Dr. A Moss
1936	Miss Peacock	1969	Mrs A.M. Robertson	1997	Mrs A.T. MacDougall
1937	Mrs Sprone	1970	Mrs J Moncrieff	1998	Mrs N.A.C. McQuade
1938	Miss Allan	1971	Mrs M Kennedy	1999	Mrs J Lawrie
1939	Miss Allan	1972	Miss M.O. McKenzie	2000	Mrs Ann Gardner
1946	Mrs J A Stewart	1973	Mrs D.P. Storey	2001	Mrs M Gray
1947	Mrs J A Stewart	1974	Mrs J.G. Budd	2002	Mrs K Thornton
1948	Mrs Dorothy Smith	1975	Mrs D Campbell	2003	Mrs Marilyn Muir
1949	Mrs Marion P Rollo	1976	Mrs I.G. Conn	2004	Mrs Valerie Clegg
1950	Mrs Jean I McQuhae	1977	Mrs D Alexander	2005	Mrs Jean Lawrie /
1951	Mrs Marion Gardner	1978	Mrs M McMaster		Mrs Marilyn Muir
1952	Mrs Catherine R Wilson	1979	Mrs J.C. McCusker		

Club Champions

1906 T Fawsitt	1940 H McMaster	1972 T.C. Houston
1907 F. H. Mingay	1941 No Comp	1973 T.C. Houston
1908 T Fawsitt	1942 No Comp	1974 Dan Campbell
1909 F. H. Mingay	1943 No Comp	1975 G.T. Edgar
1910 S Cohen	1944 No Comp	1976 R Kerr
1911 F. H. Mingay	1945 No Comp	1977 T.C. Houston
1912 A. B. Ferrie	1946 K.I. McLeod	1978 R Kerr
1913 J. W. Ferrie	1947 W.M. Muirhead	1979 Graeme Conn
1914 F. H. Mingay	1948 A.E. McLeod	1980 Allan M. Hunter
1915 No Comp	1949 W.S. McLeod	1981 T.C. Houston
1916 M Barr Jnr	1950 Alex MacPherson	1982 S.D. Thomson
1917 No Comp	1951 W.S. McLeod	1983 J.K. Gardner
1918 No Comp	1952 W.S. McLeod	1984 K Morrison
1919 J.W. Ferrie	1953 John Arnott	1985 William Young
1920 James Anderson	1954 J.L. McClue	1986 Alan H. Edgar
1921 J Anderson Jnr	1955 J.L. McClue	1987 Allan M Hunter
1922 James Carmichael	1956 J.L. McClue	1988 A.W. Kidd
1923 John Anderson	1957 J.L. McClue	1989 Allan M. Hunter
1924 R Levack	1958 J.L. McClue	1990 K Morrison
1925 John Anderson	1959 A. G. Clark	1991 H MacDonald
1926 R Levack	1960 A. G. Clark	1992 H MacDonald
1927 John Brodie/ A.E. McLeod	1961 Ian Brodie	1993 H MacDonald
1928 Ian S. McLeod	1962 T.C. Houston	1994 H MacDonald
1929 John Anderson	1963 T.C. Houston	1995 H MacDonald
1930 John Anderson	1964 J Houston	1996 H MacDonald
1931 A.E. McLeod	1965 W.C. Smith	1997 H MacDonald
1932 Alex McPherson	1966 Ian Brodie	1998 H MacDonald
1933 John Anderson	1967 A Quigg	1999 Alistair Lyle
1934 W.S. McLeod	1968 R Kerr	2000 H MacDonald
1935 D McMaster	1969 A Quigg	2001 Alistair Lyle
1936 A. E. McLeod	1970 G.R. Blair	2002 Mathew J.S. Clark
1937 H McMaster	1971 R Kerr	2003 Clark J. Taylor
1938 W. S. McLeod		2004 Alistair Lyle
1939 D McMaster		2005 G Campbell

Lady Champions

1954 Mrs D Robertson	1980 Miss W Aitken
1955 Mrs M Pryce	1981 Miss W Aitken
1956 Mrs D Robertson	1982 Miss W Aitken
1957 Mrs D Robertson	1983 Miss W Aitken
1958 Mrs D Robertson	1984 Miss W Aitken
1959 Mrs D Robertson	1985 Mrs R Anderson
1960 Mrs D Robertson	1986 Marilyn Muir
1961 Miss I H Kennedy	1987 Mrs W Leburn
1962 Mrs D Robertson	1988 Mrs W Leburn
1963 Mrs D Robertson	1989 Marilyn Muir
1964 Miss M R R Borland	1990 Marilyn Muir
1965 Miss M R R Borland	1991 Mrs W Leburn
1966 Miss M R R Borland	1992 Mrs R Anderson
1967 Miss M R R Borland	1993 Mrs F Storey
1968 Miss J Leonard	1994 Marilyn Muir
1969 Miss M R R Borland	1995 Marilyn Muir
1970 Miss J Leonard	1996 Mrs M J Dunlop
1971 Mrs D Robertson	1997 Marilyn Muir
1972 Miss I H Kennedy	1998 Mrs B Clark
1973 Miss M R R Borland	1999 Rena Anderson
1974 Mrs D Robertson	2000 Rena Anderson
1975 Miss W Aitken	2001 Margaret Robertson
1975 Miss W Aitken	2002 Marilyn Muir
1976 Miss W Aitken	2003 Marilyn Muir
1977 Miss W Aitken	2004 Marilyn Muir
1978 Miss W Aitken	2005 Ann McKenzie
1979 Miss W Aitken	

The McLeod Cup
Winners

1947 W Irvine – Pollock

1948 DS Govan – Bothwell Castle

1949 Allan Stevenson – Prestwick St Nicholas

1950 JL Hastings – Ralston

1951 JC Russell – Fereneze

1952 GB Peters – Fereneze

1953 Allan Stevenson – Prestwick St Nicholas

1954 Hamilton McInally – Irvine

1955 FWG Deighton – Hilton Park

1956 A Sinclair – West Kilbride

1957 DH Reid – Pollok

1958 SWT Murray – Old Ranfurly

1959 SWT Murray – Elderslie

1960 SWT Murray – Elderslie

1961 Iain L Rae – Greenock

1962 JA Gardner – Elderslie

1963 CW Green – Dumbarton

1964 DS Cameron – Annanhill

1965 WA Bryce – Hayston

1966 CW Green – Dumbarton

1967 CW Green – Dumbarton

1968 ID Hamilton – Troon

1969 DB Hendry – Greenock

1970 JC Fulton – Prestwick St Nicholas

1971 DB Howard – Cochrane Castle

1972 SW Gaston – Rothesay

1973 DM Robertson – Cochrane Castle

1974 R Smith – Hamilton

1975 DB Howard – Cochrane Castle

1976 DB Howard – Cochrane Castle

1977 DB Howard – Cochrane Castle

1978 CW Green – Dumbarton

1979 CW Green – Dumbarton

1980 CW Green – Dumbarton

1981 KC Ross – East Kilbride

1982 KC Ross – East Kilbride

1983 KC Ross – East Kilbride

1984 JP Davis – Ranfurly Castle

1985 JLS Kinloch – Cardross

1986 JLS Kinloch – Cardross

1987 RSS Millar – Cochrane Castle

1988 RSS Millar – Cochrane Castle

1989 A Tait – Bogside

1990 D Robertson – Cochrane Castle

1991 GA Crawford – Williamwood

1992 H MacDonald – Old Ranfurly

1993 H MacDonald – Old Ranfurly

1994 H MacDonald – Old Ranfurly

1995 H MacDonald – Old Ranfurly

1996 G Rankin – Palacerigg

1997 G Rankin - Palacerigg

Junior Champions

1960 B Beeton	1983 I McKendrick
1961 I Wylie	1984 M Sharp
1962 N McNair	1985 A Edgar
1963 A Quigg	1986 B Lind
1964 N McNair	1987 S Hunter
1965 N.J.McNair	1988 R Craig
1966 W Barnaby	1989 M Robb
1967 ———————	1990 A Campbell
1968 G Whiteford	1991 A Campbell
1969 G Whiteford	1992 P Taylor
1970 A Niven	1993 B Welsford
1971 K Smith	1994 G Miller
1972 P Fife	1995 G Webster
1973 A Campbell	1996 A Dundas
1974 A Campbell	1997 A Moss
1975 N McCaffrey	1998 M Clark
1976 D Conn	1999 M Clark
1977 A Sutherland	2000 G Jamieson
1978 P Davis	2001 C Burns
1979 A.S. Corstorphine	2002 D Lawson
1980 S Agnew	2003 C Michael
1981 S.D. Thompson	2004 D Lawson
1982 S.A. Murphy	2005 J Binning

Old Ranfurly Secretaries

1905 – 1916:-   Mr John Macfarlane

1916 – 1941:-   Mr William G Millar

1941 – 1942:-   Mr Matthew Barr

1942 – 1946:-   Mr Harold Walker

1946 – 1951:-   Mr Hugh McMaster

1951 – 1953:-   Mr John Hall

1953 – 1960:-   Mr George Barr

1960 – 1968:-   Mr George T. Smith

1968 – 1970:-   Wg/Cmdr A. G. Murray

1970 – 1973:-   Mr Frank Charteris

1973 – 1974:-   Mr Alistair T. Moncrieff

1974 – 1975:-   Mr George T. Smith

1975 – 1990:-   Mr Ronald McCallum

1990 – 1991:-   Mr J. B. Wilson

1990 – 1998:-   Mr Robert Mitchell

1998 – 1999:-   Mr Kenneth Young

2000 -   Mr Quintin J. McClymont

Further Reading

Books referred to while researching were:-

Ranfurly Castle Golf Club – A Centenary History by Robert Crampsey

Western Gailes 1897 – 1997

The Breezy Links o' Troon – A History of Royal Troon Golf Club by Robert Crampsey

The Centenary History of Cochrane Castle Golf Club by W.F. Mitchell

The Dawn of Professional Golf by Peter N. Lewis

The Golfer's Handbook (various years but the older ones are far more interesting)

Morton Greats by Graeme Ross

Erskine Golf Club by Ron Garrett

The History of Port Glasgow Golf Club by I. George

Acknowledgements

To the Captain and Directors of the Old Course Ranfurly Golf I must convey my thanks for entrusting me with the recording of the first one hundred years of the Club's history.

To the Centenary Committee of Bobby Murdoch, Peter Herbert, Marilyn Muir and previously Jean Lawrie, Stuart Gray and Andrew Gardner I thank you for your continued support, advice and encouragement throughout this project.

To Jean Lawrie, for her tireless work in logging and recording all the artefacts that came my way, I am indebted.

My thanks go to the Secretary, Quintin McClymont, and to Aileen Wilson for their ever prompt responses and helpfulness to my numerous enquiries.

I am fully appreciative of the immense contribution by Kenneth Morrison who would query and enhance each piece in equal measure.

To Alyson Creighton and Nicola Watt my thanks are due for your editing, correcting and general improvement of each article.

To Linda Jackson for advice, instruction and inspiration

The hours that I spent with Walter and Kenneth McLeod I savoured immensely. Their contribution to this book is far greater than either of them appreciate.

To my friend Dan Campbell I offer my sincerest thanks for his never less than honest appraisals and constant support.

My appreciation goes also to Gavin Young and Alan Brown for their photographic work and advice.

Thanks are due to the editor of the Paisley and Renfrewshire Gazette. To the staff at Bridge of Weir Library, Paisley Central Library, the Mitchell Library and the Watt Library, Greenock, I thank them all for their genuine interest and advice.

To everyone who entrusted me any sort of memorabilia or photographs. To those who spared the time to talk with me. To those who wrote to me or e-mailed me I offer my most humble thanks. You know who you are.

To those who deserve a note in the pages of this book and who I have failed to mention, and there will be many many, I offer my most humble apologies. You know who you are also and your contribution to the good of this Golf Club will hopefully already be enshrined in the hearts of your friends.

My thanks go also to the management and staff at J McCormick, printers of Glasgow. Their professionalism and skill was delightful to experience.

And finally, I only hope that anyone reading this book will somehow manage to derive from it even a small portion of the pleasure that I have had in writing it.

Drew McKenzie
Kilmacolm, 25th October 2005

Index

The Author

Drew McKenzie is a freelance writer and lives in Kilmacolm. He has been a member of the Old Course Ranfurly Golf Club since 1987.